introducing

HALLE BERRY

ALSO BY CHRISTOPHER JOHN FARLEY

Aaliyah: More Than a Woman

My Favorite War

introducing

HALLE
BERRY

A BIOGRAPHY

CHRISTOPHER JOHN FARLEY

POCKET BOOKS

New York   London   Toronto   Sydney   Singapore

An *Original* Publication of POCKET BOOKS

 POCKET BOOKS, a division of Simon & Schuster, Inc.
1230 Avenue of the Americas, New York, NY 10020

ISBN: 0-7434-6453-2

First Pocket Books printing November 2002

10 9 8 7 6 5 4 3 2 1

POCKET and colophon are registered trademarks of
Simon & Schuster, Inc.

For information regarding special discounts for bulk purchases,
please contact Simon & Schuster Special Sales at 1-800-456-6798
or business@simonandschuster.com

Cover photo © Paul Fenton/Shooting Star

Printed in the U.S.A.

For Dylan, Obadiah, Elisha, and Sarah

Perhaps all the dragons in our lives are princesses
who are only waiting to see us act, just once,
with beauty and courage. Perhaps everything
that frightens us is, in its deepest essence,
something helpless that wants our love.

—RAINER MARIA RILKE,
"Letters to a Young Poet"

"Fantasy is what people want
but reality is what they need."

—LAURYN HILL

Contents

introducing

HALLE BERRY

Introduction,
or an Unfinished Story

THIS IS A STORY ABOUT BEAUTY AND UGLINESS, A STORY about love and pain, a true fable about seeming coincidence and apparent fate. This is also a book about black and white—not so much about the opposing shades as their mixture; it's also a look at Hollywood, the dream factory of legend, and Hollywouldn't, the mass marketer of racial and sexual stereotype. This is also a study of great fame and its opposite, total anonymity, as well as renown's evil twin, tabloid-driven infamy. In the end (and at the beginning and all throughout) it is one woman's story, but it could have been anyone's story— anyone with the courage to try, the talent to succeed, and a bit of serendipity. The French philosopher and mathematician Blaise Pascal once said "a man does not show his greatness by being at one extremity, but rather by touching both at once." Halle Berry stands astride extremes in American life.

But beyond all the fancy talk, this is just a book about a talented, good-looking movie star whom lots of people like.

I've written about Halle several times throughout her career. I interviewed her for *USA Today* in November 1991, back when she was an entertainment newcomer making her first films *Jungle Fever* and *Strictly Business*. A year later I profiled her at greater length when she landed the lead role in the television miniseries *Queen*. And I wrote about her once more for *Time* magazine after her Oscar win for best actress in 2002. The very first time I talked to her, before she was a household name, before she had been nominated for an Oscar much less won the award, before she had been linked to celebrities such as baseball star David Justice and singer Eric Benet, she was already getting a bit of motion sickness from the pace of her career. "The last year of my life," Berry told me in 1991, "has moved very, very fast."

The Hollywood establishment is primarily interested in young women—the younger the better. While male stars are allowed to age—Arnold Schwarzenegger, Clint Eastwood, Warren Beatty, Harrison Ford, and other golden oldies have continued to nab lead roles in big-budget films well into their senior years—female actresses must remain forever young. Aging male actors (like Woody Allen) continually cast much younger women to star opposite them (Allen's last few leading ladies include Tea Leoni (born 1966), Debra Messing (born 1968), and Tiffani-Amber Thiessen (born 1974), each of whom is three or four decades his junior (Allen: born 1935). According to a survey by the Screen Actors Guild in 2002, although almost half of all women in the United

States are *over* forty, almost 80 percent of female roles in Hollywood movies are filled by women *under* forty.

The film industry, therefore, has an insatiable need for ingenues. Every week there's another fresh, pretty face playing the love interest opposite some established male star. Every month we see one of those same fresh, pretty faces staring out from some glossy magazine like *Maxim*, or *FHM*, or *Vanity Fair*. We remember the names of these young women for a minute or so, and then we move on, and so does Hollywood. When one looks back through film history, it's sad, but not surprising, to see just how many female up-and-comers have gone-and-went after high-profile releases.

The following women, once on Hollywood's "A" list, have pretty much fallen off the alphabet:

- Maria Schneider, who got all buttered up with Marlon Brando in *Last Tango in Paris* (1972).
- Karen Allen, co-star, along with Harrison Ford, of *Raiders of the Lost Ark* (1981).
- Alison Doody, who co-starred with Ford in *Indiana Jones and the Last Crusade* (1989).
- Valeria Golino, who co-starred with Tom Cruise in *Rain Man* (1988).
- Tia Carrere, co-star, along with Mike Myers, of *Wayne's World* (1992).
- Julia Ormond, who starred opposite Brad Pitt in *Legends of the Fall* (1994).
- Claire Forlani, who starred opposite Pitt in *Meet Joe Black* (1998).

The men these women performed alongside are still stars, but the women themselves, if not completely forgotten, are currently struggling for character parts in made-for-cable pictures and the like. Hollywood, when it comes to women, loves to make an introduction, delights in parading new, previously unseen female flesh across the screen. But once the camera penetrates and deflowers, Hollywood rolls over, sated and uninterested and imagining new conquests. The film industry, when it comes to female stars, requires virgin sacrifices.

In my initial interview with Halle, back in 1991, she made it clear that she understood Hollywood's rules— and that she was going to do everything possible *not* to play by them, and to not let them play her. One might expect an actress new to the film industry to have nothing but good things to say about the business, especially to a national publication like *USA Today*, especially because the people she might work with, the people who are in a position to hire and fire her, might be reading. Halle pulled no punches. "My role in *Strictly Business* was underwritten," she told me, criticizing her latest release while it was still in theaters. But she wasn't done yet—she went on to take a shot at an upcoming movie she was in co-starring Damon Wayans and Bruce Willis. "Even my role in *The Last Boy Scout* was underwritten," Halle said. "It's frustrating."

Halle continued. She had lots of gripes, but she wasn't just about sitting on the sidelines and complaining. She was taking action to try to shape her own career in the way she saw fit. Halle told me her role models were strong successful women; females who wouldn't take no for an answer and wouldn't always give a meek yes in reply. She looked up to Jodie Foster, because she was an actress who had taken on diverse roles and also branched out successfully in producing and directing. Halle also said she was an admirer of black activist/sixties radical Angela Davis, and dreamed of someday portraying her on screen.

Halle, inspired by such women, saw Hollywood's many problems not as a mere barrier, but as a challenge. In fact, she was writing her own screenplays and was shopping them around. "That's what inspired me to write my own things," she said. "That way, I'm in control, I'm holding the pen and paper. Black women need to put energy into their own projects—like Spike Lee."

In his 1976 nonfiction book about the film industry, *The Devil Finds Work,* James Baldwin wrote that "It is said that the camera cannot lie, but rarely do we allow it to do anything else, since the camera sees what you point it at: the camera sees what you want it to see. The language of the camera is the language of our dreams." But the question is: Whose dreams are up there on screen? Are they our dreams, the fantasies of ordinary Americans, blacks and whites and Hispanics and Asians, men and women, middle class and working class?

Baldwin was headed in the right direction with his reasoning, but reached the wrong conclusion. The language of the camera is the language of *someone else's* dream. It can be a sweet reprise, to spend two hours in the cool dark, caught up in someone else's imagination—

to ride across the moon with *E.T.: The Extra-Terrestrial* or go martial-arts fighting in *Crouching Tiger, Hidden Dragon*. But Hollywood can, just as easily, and perhaps more often, engineer a hostile takeover of our imagination, offering up stereotype as truth. *Gone With the Wind* (1939), a movie many consider a classic, fostered a factually incorrect and morally offensive view of slaves (who weren't as happy as they were in that movie) and of the South (the confederate soldiers, who were, in essence, fighting to keep black people enslaved, weren't necessarily the virtuous lads they were portrayed as in the film).

Filmmakers—actors, directors, screenwriters, producers—express their personalities through their works, and often give us an intimate look into their subconscious in ways even they may not have expected, predicted, or even understand. People who are abused as children, or who suffer some sort of childhood trauma, often find themselves, again and again, reliving the event in their imaginations, or somehow constructing their lives in a way in which some version of the event is replayed over and over. Abusive husbands are often the products of abusive parents.

Sigmund Freud wrote about a woman haunted by a wedding night trauma. This woman finds herself mysteriously and neurotically running from room to room in her house and, in each room, ringing a bell and calling for a housemaid. Ten years before, the woman had married a much older man who could not perform on their wedding night, but kept coming back into the room time and time again to try once more.

Actors' lives are like that—they are the ultimate neurotics. Actors live out past problems again and again, and call it their work. On stage, actors play out traumas once a day, with matinees on Wednesdays and Saturdays. In films, actors experience traumas again and again as they pace through their scenes, sometimes performing the same lines dozens of times. Sometimes the work actors do merely represents the personal problems of the playwright, screenwriter, or director. Other times, in works of significance such as *The Crucible,* or *Angels in America,* the trauma portrayed may represent something national or universal in scope.

In his book *The Hero and the Blues,* the novelist and cultural critic Albert Murray writes that "Storybook images are indispensable to the basic human process of world comprehension and self-definition (and hence personal motivation as well as purposeful group behavior) as are the formulas of physical science or the nomenclature of the social sciences." In other words, there's a formula on how to live to be gotten out of every poem, every book, every play, and every movie. Perhaps the theme for *Rambo: First Blood* might be $V + P = A$, where V = violence, P = patriotism, and A = America.

Halle Berry has given the world a new kind of formula. She's offered her viewers, and the world, a different way of looking at women and looking at life. Just as Oprah Winfrey's book club choices tended to follow a certain pattern and explored certain themes (women in peril, abused children, societal ills, etc.), Berry's film choices have also fallen along certain lines. She has made some films that have been great, and some that have been dogs, but her choices have been richer and more varied than those of almost any black actress who came before her and almost any other actress, black or white, who is her contemporary.

There are two types of performers working in Hollywood: There are actors and there are stars. Julia Roberts is a star. Meryl Streep is an actress. Tom Cruise is a star. Daniel Day-Lewis is an actor. Actors immerse themselves in any given role, adopting accents and mannerisms, and are often unrecognizable in the parts they choose. Stars always play themselves. Every time we see a star's movie, we know what we're getting: a Julia Roberts movie or a Sandra Bullock movie or a Tom Cruise movie. Their characters, inevitably, react in ways we've come to expect from the particular actor or actress in question. If it's a Clint Eastwood movie, the character is going to squint a lot and, at some point, shoot all the bad guys. If it's a Mel Gibson movie, at some point Mel will get tortured by the bad guys only to take his righteous revenge later, firing off manly wisecracks all the way. If it's an Eddie Murphy flick, he'll adopt different personas to fast talk himself out of jams. And so on. The situations vary from movie to movie but the star never does. That why they're stars—they are constant and untouchable and you can steer by them.

Halle Berry, along with Denzel Washington, Russell Crowe, and perhaps Johnny Depp, is one of a handful of stars who are also actors. Berry is glamorous and stylish—but she's not afraid to take on roles that contradict her public image. She's made those kinds of hard, challenging choices from the beginning of her career, when she played a crack addict in Spike Lee's *Jungle Fever* (1991). Her characters are beautiful (after all she's playing them), but not always glamorous; her acting style is often affable, but with a muted rage that sometimes bursts out and makes itself known. In her work, she seems to beckon us to peek beneath the surface of things—beneath smiles, beneath beauty, beneath skin. She has refused to be ruled, in her on-screen choices, by her race, her beauty, or her sex—and in doing so, she has opened up a world of possibilities to anyone who experiences her work. If Halle can dream herself out of the boundaries society has attempted to set for her, then why can't we?

In 1999, Diana Ross complained to me that even after she had scored major successes in the 1970s with *Lady Sings the Blues* (1972) and *Mahogany* (1975), she wasn't offered the plum parts, the good scripts, the major roles, and her acting career withered. Halle's very first role after her Oscar-winning turn in *Monster's Ball* was a part in the spy thriller *Die Another Day* as a Bond girl—a movie franchise that eats new actresses alive, introducing a fresh new face every installment and promptly replacing the newcomer, whoever she is, in the inevitable sequel. Only the man—Sean Connery in the past, Pierce Brosnan currently—gets to make multiple starring appearances in the Bond series: perhaps no franchise could be more symbolic of the way Hollywood works. While there's no particular shame in playing a Bond girl—Kim Basinger was a Bond girl, too—it's not necessarily going to set you up for more work and it probably won't put you in position for another Oscar.

But, as we will see, Halle had her reasons for taking a part in a Bond film.

Will Berry be able to build on her past successes? She's in her mid-thirties, a dangerous time for any actress. Established male stars may start to look past her, searching for younger faces in the crowds of the undiscovered.

But Berry's story is still unfinished. This is how it starts . . .

"I don't care what is written about
me so long as it isn't true."

—KATHARINE HEPBURN

"I've forgiven him, but I haven't forgotten.
I have no love for him, because he is a complete
stranger. I don't want him to be part of my life.
I don't know him and I don't owe him anything."

—HALLE BERRY ON HER FATHER

ONE

Shades of Meaning

A dog is flying across the room. It's Oscar time. The night of nights. The starriest evening of the year, even in a town like Hollywood—known for constellations. Tom Hanks is here. Mel Gibson. Denzel Washington. Will Smith. Julia Roberts. But there is only one woman in the spotlight right now: Halle Berry. Tears are running down her cheeks. Her neck is tight with emotion. In her left hand she clutches the Academy Award for best actress. It is the first ever given to a woman of color. She holds it tight as if someone might take it away from her, even now, even in front of the hundreds of stars in the audience, the thousands of ordinary spectators, the millions of television viewers. But there is a dog flying across the room. She is thinking about her family. All the struggle, all the pain, all the setbacks—it's all coming back, as if it never left. She pays tribute to her mother, her husband, her stepchild. She also pays homage to her father—but not the one who was her biological parent. Berry calls her manager, Vincent Cirrincione, the man who helped guide her career for twelve years, "the only father I've ever known." Halle is a true child of showbiz now. The past is past. But that dog, its tongue bleeding red, continues its flight across the room.

The beginning wasn't pretty. It's hard to look at Halle Berry now—the bright hopeful eyes, the perfectly tousled hair, the smile as white as clouds on a sunny day— and imagine that her story started with so much ugliness. Even now she has grotesque memories: of screams and slaps, of fights at the dining room table, of battles between her mother and father. When I first talked to Halle in 1991, I expected her to talk only of pretty things: her red-hot career, her looks, fashion, other beautiful movie folks. Instead, she had ugliness on her mind: the pressures of working in Hollywood, the difficulty of being a woman in the film industry, the barriers faced by actors of color, and the racism she had faced her entire life because she was a black woman. "I got called 'Zebra' and 'Oreo' in school," she told me.

Halle was born into struggle. It's the mid-1960s. J.F.K. has already been assassinated; M.L.K. is about to be. It is illegal in sixteen states for blacks and whites to marry each other. In places around the South, blacks and whites use separate rest rooms; in places around the North, blacks and whites attend separate public schools (that part is still true). But at the movies—a projection of hope perhaps or an outlet for social fantasy—there are some encouraging trends. At the Academy Awards for 1963, Sidney Poitier wins the Best Actor Oscar for his performance in *Lilies of the Field* as a journeyman who meets up with a group of nuns. He is the first African American ever to win the award. It would be four more decades before an African-American woman would follow suit.

Around the same time, in the mid-1960s, against the odds, against prevailing social trends, against the wishes of their parents, a white woman and a black man fall in love in Cleveland, Ohio. Her name is Judith Hawkins and she is a nurse in a psychiatric hospital; his name is Jerome Berry, and he is a nurse's aide in that same hospital. Judith was a native of Liverpool, England, but left when she was ten and grew up in the suburb of Elyria, Ohio. The two begin to date and are soon married; in 1966 they have their first child together, a daughter they name Heide. Then, on August 14, 1966, the couple has their second and final child together: a daughter they name Halle. It is an unusual name for a baby who will go on to have an extraordinary career. "My mother was shopping in Halle Brothers in Cleveland," Berry was quoted as saying by the Knight Ridder/Tribune News Service in 2000. "She saw their bags and thought, 'That's what I'm going to name my child.' No one ever says it right. It's *Halle*, like *Sally*." She was given the middle name of Maria.

Cleveland, with all due respect, is not the kind of place one expects legends to be born. It is, however, part of a region that has given birth to its share of American presidents: William Henry Harrison, Benjamin Harrison, William Howard Taft, and William Harding all hail from the state. The Buckeye State has also given rise to a number of other luminaries, including Olympic athlete Jesse Owens, singer Tracy Chapman, and talk-show host Phil Donahue. More on point, a number of notable actors come from Cleveland, including Ruby Dee, Hal Holbrook, and Debra Winger. "I come from humble, humble beginnings," Halle told the *Cleveland Plain Dealer* in 1997. "One mother and two latchkey kids. We went without a whole lot of things; we had the bare essentials, but for the most part we struggled. . . . So I can understand having big dreams and little money, and no way of knowing how you're gonna make 'em come true. Most definitely."

Halle said to London's *Daily Mail* in 1993: "I think being raised by a single parent was important for me because I saw the struggle. I don't believe all that Hollywood hype that goes with this business. I know I'm only as good and as bad as the last film I just did and people don't care about me. If someone chooses to put me in a movie it's because they think I can make them money. It's not because of Halle Berry."

Cleveland has been in economic decline since perhaps the 1970s. Around 20 percent of all Ohio residents are employed in manufacturing. But sometime around the date of Halle's birth, the economic character of the state began to change. The factories in the area had become old and inefficient, having failed to modernize and keep up with the times. Every few years, someone in Ohio or in Washington, D.C., announces that there's a new boom under way in the Rust Belt states or that some economic miracle is just around the corner, but the truth is the region is still, at the time of this writing, immersed in a slump.

Cleveland should be beautiful. The name "Ohio" is a French adaptation of a Seneca-Iroquois word meaning "beautiful river." Cleveland should rock—it claims to be the birthplace of rock 'n' roll and is home to the Rock and Roll Hall of Fame and Museum. Cleveland should be a haven for African Americans. It was a hub for runaway slaves seeking freedom on the Underground Railroad during slavery, and several Union generals, including Ulysses S. Grant and William Tecumseh Sherman, hail from Ohio. The state was also once home to Harriet Beecher Stowe, the woman who wrote the abolitionist novel *Uncle Tom's Cabin.* But Cleveland is also, infamously, the place where a river caught fire. In 1972, the Cuyahoga River, which had become choked with industrial pollution, burst into flames. As for music, Cleveland hasn't launched a significant new rock act in years.

In terms of race relations, young Halle found that her city and state had a long way to go. She also found, early on, that she had to deal with racial issues without being able to rely on her father for help or advice. Jerome Berry left his young family when Halle was four years old. According to Halle, her father was abusive—to her, to her sister, to her mother, and even to himself. "He was an alcoholic, he battered my mother," Halle said to *People* in 1996. "I haven't had much to do with him." Halle was also left with familial guilt—could she have done more to stop his rampages? Obviously, because she was only a small child, she couldn't have done anything, but guilt, and memory, work in strange ways. "He beat my mom and my sister," Halle told the *New York Times* in 2002. "He threw our dog against the wall. He never hit me. I felt a lot of guilt. When my sister saw him hitting my mother, she would jump in and get hit, but I would run and hide. I got out of the way."

Strangely, Halle seems to have transferred some culpability for her father's abuse onto her sister—Halle and Heidi are reportedly estranged, and do not talk regularly or have a close relationship. Halle told *Movieline* in December 2001/January 2002: "We fought a lot. I don't know but part of me feels we never recovered from the adolescent years. We fought for real. Sometimes drawing blood. I moved away from home at such a young age that the relationship never quite repaired itself."

The first time I talked to Halle in 1991, I was struck by how immediate, how palpable, the pain and turmoil of her childhood still seems to her. It was one of the first subjects she brought up, and it was raised with little prompting from me. Perhaps being upfront about her background is her way of dealing with it. One of her high school classmates told me that not long after she met Halle for the first time, Halle broke out pictures of her parents and explained that they were of different races. Images from her family turmoil still haunt her, particularly the dog-tossing incident. In the *Mirror* in 2002, Halle was quoted as saying "We had a toy Maltese and my father threw it across the dining room at dinner and the dog almost bit its tongue off." That's a scene that's hard to forget. Halle went on: "The blood and that image. When somebody mentions my father, that's the first thing I think about—that dog flying across the room. I remember crying: 'God, let him leave!' so that my life could get back to normal."

But when one is raised in such circumstances, what is normal? Sometimes dysfunction, eventually, inevitably, becomes the accepted, even longed-for, state of affairs. After their first breakup, Halle's parents got back together for one year in 1976. It was an optimistic year: the national nightmare of Watergate was receding; Jimmy Carter, with his big peanut-farmer smile, had taken the White House; and the whole U.S.A. was gearing up to celebrate the bicentennial. At the movies, *Rocky* had grabbed the Academy Award for best picture and George Lucas was putting the finishing touches on his escapist sci-fi classic *Star Wars*.

Perhaps caught up in the general spirit of optimism, Judith Berry took Jerome Berry back. The experiment failed and the family split up again within a year. Halle, who, in his absence, had idealized her father to a certain extent, in part because she didn't really know him, was forced to deal with the reality of who he was. It was a crushing time. "I had longed for my father a lot until that time," Halle told *InStyle* in July 2000. "But he was not the image I had made my daddy out to be. If I had lived with him any longer that year, I know I would have turned out to be a very different kind of person."

Halle confided to London's *Daily Mail* in 1993 that she thought her father's drinking was a root cause of her family's turmoil. "My mother couldn't deal with it and he left. He came back a few years later but he wasn't any better. He was like a stranger to us and then he just disappeared. I see his mother, my grandmother, and he contacts her once in a while. She tells me he's still an alcoholic, and he's been into every drug going. I'd like to help him but I don't think he would appreciate me doing that, plus I haven't the slightest idea how to get in contact with him."

Later, when Halle was twenty-two years old and a young adult, she met up with her father again. This time, she said, she "felt nothing." But the nothingness was a cover for a complex tangle of feelings. In an interview with the *Washington Post* in 1999 she explained her feelings more fully: "I realized that I always had a feeling of not being enough and that came from my father leaving. It came from so many things that I never felt good enough. I really suffered from low self-esteem for many years."

Later in life Halle came to realize that her relationship, or lack of one, with her father had poisoned her relationship with men. It made her reach out, time and time again, for men who were wrong for her, who disrespected her, who were abusive in varying ways. Halle told the *Express* in 2002: "I equated that kind of behavior with love."

Jerome Berry is said to have fallen mortally ill. He is reportedly suffering from Parkinson's disease. One member of the Berry clan told me that making up with Halle "is his main goal. I think that's what he's living for—the day she walks in his room. He wants to apologize to her.

Because he doesn't understand the anger that's in her that's against him."

Reconciliation, however, doesn't seem to be in the immediate future. "I've forgiven him, but I haven't forgotten," Berry told the *Mirror* in 2002. "I have no love for him, because to me he is a complete stranger. I don't want him to be part of my life. I don't know him and I don't owe him anything."

One of the worst things any estranged parent can do is to reach out to a child after that son or daughter has made it big. Success doesn't diminish loss, it magnifies it; when one is forced to succeed without a parent, every dollar one earns, every accolade one receives, arrives with this underlying feeling: *I did this without my father or mother. Damn him. Damn her.* The damnation is cumulative and damaging. Fame and fortune, instead of being things one revels in, become things that force one to revisit one's root loss—and to curse it all over again. When Halle and her father crossed paths after she had become a star, rage seemed to always be close behind— even when their involvement was only from afar. "I have no contact with my father," Halle told the *New York Times* in 2001. "A few years ago he sold a story to *The Star* about me for a six-pack of beer. I thought, If you're going to sell the damn story, then at least make some real money."

Judith moved her family out to the predominately white Cleveland suburb of Oakwood Village when Halle was ten years old. But there were tensions there as well. As

Halle mingled with other children in school, she soon discovered that the things she took for granted—like having parents of two different races—were, to some, controversial. And early on, her fellow students introduced her to racial intolerance. Halle told Barbara Walters in 2002: "Yeah, I think probably when I was in the third grade and it was from another kid at school who had gotten a glimpse of my mother and told me that she couldn't possibly be my mother because had I noticed that she was white and I wasn't."

Rage and questions of race were often intermingled. Even with Halle's father out of the picture, there were other things that sparked emotional outbursts—and they often had to do with racial confrontations. "I remember the fury my mother would feel in line at the grocery store because people around us assumed that these black kids couldn't possibly be her children," Halle told the *Daily Telegraph* (London) in 2002.

In July 2002 I talked to one of Halle's Bedford High School classmates, Stacy Lavinsky. Halle and Lavinsky met in tenth grade in a Spanish class. Their mothers knew each other a bit and that helped the kids to develop a friendship. Lavinsky was always curious about the life of models and, at the time, Halle was also giving the profession a lot of thought, and so the two frequently talked about the subject. Lavinsky, who is white, says it was difficult to strike up an interracial friendship at Bedford High at the time. Racial boundaries at the school were lines that were not to be crossed. Says Lavinksy: "It was extremely hard to get along. There was a lot of racism going on between the blacks and the whites. This is from my perspective."

It was during this period that Halle developed a personal trait that would serve to both undermine some of her future relationships and also help to propel her to the top of her chosen profession. At her new school, in her new town, she felt isolated and anomalous. Even as she endured the stares and half-heard some of the taunts, a desire began to grow in her: She wanted to find ways to demonstrate her talent, and her worth, to everyone around her. This yearning for acceptance and acknowledgment would drive her all her life. It was, like other primal wants—for air, for food—something that could be temporarily satisfied but never completely sated. It was an enormous, insatiable need. "I was one of only three or four black high school kids, and I felt the need to prove I was as smart as everyone else," Halle told the publication *Scotland on Sunday* in 2000. "After high school, I was worn out with proving and working. It felt like I had a day job in high school. Trying to be Miss Everything." Halle disclosed to the *New York Times* in 1995: "It was sickening how much I craved being liked. I was Miss Everything—cheerleader, student senator, on the newspaper, the honor roll, you name it."

With only one overworked parent around to care for her, Halle was left largely untutored in a number of important personal development areas. Love was one of them. Halle told the British edition of *Glamour* in July 2002 that when she was seven or eight she began asking her mother all the inevitable questions about where babies come from. Her mother sat her down and, along with Halle, paged through some books about the subject. Young Halle, confronted with the facts, thought: "That's gotta really hurt. Why would anybody want to do that?" Her mother didn't answer—probably because she knew that, in time, Halle would find out for herself. Another area in which Halle's education was lacking was in the topic of race. Jerome Berry, despite his failings, might have been able to tell her about her background. Had he stayed in the picture, he might have been able to explain to her the burdens and hardships of being African American, the challenges, the history, the racist barriers. But he wasn't there, and the only parent Halle had left, Judith Berry, couldn't tell her that much about being African American or even American, given the fact that she was born neither. "My father left Mom with two little black kids," Halle was quoted as saying in 2000. "She supported us working as a nurse in a psychiatric hospital and I saw her go through a lot of pain." Halle so admired her mom that when Halle was ten she wanted to be a psychiatrist because, at the time, her mother was a nurse on the psych ward of a veteran's hospital.

In the movies, race mixing is often depicted as difficult, tragic, even life-threatening. In *Imitation of Life* (1934; remade in 1959), a light-skinned woman who passes for white is portrayed as confused and sad. In the musical *West Side Story* (1961), a love affair between a white man and a Puerto Rican woman (played by the not-at-all Puerto Rican Natalie Wood) ends in death and bloodshed. Fictional movies about racial mixing sometimes generate strong real-world response: When the film *Island in the Sun* (1957), which co-stars Dorothy Dandridge and depicts (rather benignly) interracial affairs, was first released, the South Carolina legislature considered fining any theater that screened it $5,000; Darryl Zanuck, the producer, announced he'd pay any and all penalties himself; the South Carolina legislature eventually backed down.

Halle cut through all the negative messages about race-mixing in the media all around her and drew her own conclusions about who she was. "Being the product of an interracial marriage, I've always known the racial divide is insane and ridiculous," she told the *Los Angeles Times* in 2002. And Halle's mother pointed her daughter in the right direction. "I am white and you are black," Halle's mother told her. Judith didn't want Halle living an in-between life, an existence in the margins, belonging to two races and being wanted or claimed by neither. Halle was quoted as saying in 2000: "[My mother] taught me to identify myself as black because that's what people see. Mom said, 'Be glad you're different.' She told me I was God's special child. I could have looked like dirt on a shoe and she would have put me on a pedestal."

Halle told me in 1991 that one reason she thought of herself as black is that she didn't want to end up like the mixed-race folks she saw in the popular media. She didn't want an "imitation of life," she wanted the real thing, the whole thing, and she wanted to break free of all the images and stereotypes that were associated with kids with parents of different races. She said to me, "I see people on talk shows who are mixed and they seem very confused." She didn't feel confused, not about race. She looked black and she felt black. Her racial identity would be one constant in her life.

America is, of course, a racially mixed country. And in recent years, as the number of interracial marriages has climbed, there are more Americans who can claim mixed race ancestry. The fact is, though, that things are even more blended than they seem. While only people who look partially "black" are considered to be of mixed race, the truth is, many so-called white Americans actually have black ancestry and just don't know it or haven't thought to check. According to molecular anthropologist Mark D. Shriver, more than fifty million "white" Americans have at least one black ancestor. In other words, about 30 percent of whites in America are actually partially black but just don't know it.

In addition, at the turn of the millennium, public acceptance of interracial marriages is at record levels. A 1997 Gallup poll found that 77 percent of blacks and 61 percent of whites approve of such unions. Multiracial stars are all over the media, from golfer Tiger Woods to actor Vin Diesel to NBA star Jason Kidd to singers Mariah Carey, Christina Aguilera, and Alicia Keys. Taking her mother's advice, Halle took a stand in her own life that differed from multiracial stars such as Tiger Woods, who has described himself as "Cablinasian" and who doesn't view himself as black, white, or Asian. Halle told *Ebony* in 1992: "I think the problems are made worse when people get on talk shows and make statements like 'I had a hard time because I was caught in the middle.' It doesn't have to be that way. I think being biracial is one of the best things in the world." Since she was a little girl, Halle has thought of herself as one thing: black.

People have a right to define themselves, and it's difficult for anyone to say what the right choice in such matters should be, but Halle's decision certainly can be described as a brave one, and it was a signal of things to come. Her choice showed that she was a woman who was prepared to take a difficult path, even if easier roads were stretched before her; her choice sent a message that she was prepared to embrace outsider culture, even if she was offered an inside track. "Sure, I can say that I'm biracial, and technically I am," Halle told *Ebony*. "But as my mother said to me: 'What do you see when you look in the mirror? You see what everyone else sees. They don't know you're biracial. They don't know who your mother is, and they aren't going to care.'"

Interestingly, Halle didn't view her racial identity as a choice; she saw it as something she had to accept, like her height or the color of her eyes. Halle told *Movieline* in 2002: "It's not a choice you make. For me to sit here and say, 'I feel white,' somebody would try and commit me somewhere. When people see me, nobody ever thinks I'm white. No person in my whole life has ever thought that I was white. As I've gotten older people have thought I was Mexican or Chicano or Italian even. But never white, and not connected to anything ... Kids are cruel. . . . They're spewing out the views of their parents; they often don't even know what they're saying."

Halle also told the *Atlanta Journal-Constitution* in 2002: "The great thing about my mother is that even though she was white, she was really concerned about what would happen to me as I grew up as a black woman in this country. She taught me a lot about my history, where I came from and how to maybe deal with racism. Don't get mad about it, don't get militant about it, but make quiet change, you know. Live a good life and work hard at whatever I decide to do. And that's the best revenge, to succeed in this country where maybe people don't want to see us as a race succeed."

W.E.B. DuBois once said that the chief challenge of the twentieth century would be "the color line." The color line has continued to pose a challenge in the twenty-first century. One of the main problems is that the line doesn't really exist. Race doesn't exist. *Racism* exists, of course, but race itself is a social fiction. Cultures exist—blacks created the blues, jazz, rock 'n' roll, and hip-hop. A complete list of black cultural accomplishments could fill not only this book, but several volumes and several libraries besides. But race as a scientific measure is really just a fiction.

In his book *The Emperor's New Clothes: Biological Theories of Race at the Millennium,* Joseph L. Graves Jr., a professor of evolutionary biology at Arizona State University, argues that race, as a scientific concept, is a fraud. "The term 'race' implies the existence of some nontrivial underlying hereditary features shared by a group of people and not present in other groups," he writes. "None of the physical features by which we have historically defined human races—skin color, hair type, body stature, blood groups, disease prevalence—unambiguously corresponds to the racial groups that we have constructed." In other words, all the shorthand things we use to define the races are bunk—some Italians have dark skin that looks "African," some Hispanics have eyes that look "Asian," some Blacks have straight hair that looks "white." Although Graves debunks race as a valid scientific construct, he is quick to point out that prejudice is nonetheless a major problem in American life: "Clearly, recognizing that no biological races exist in our species cannot be confused with claiming that socially defined racism has not existed and is not still a problem."

Halle, as a child, felt the sting of prejudice. "I got the name-calling, Oreo, that kind of thing," she told the *Atlanta Journal-Constitution* in 1994. "I had a rough childhood." At one point, she even wondered whether she was adopted. She thought that because "when enough little kids tell you that you can't possibly be your mother's because she's white . . . what they say means a lot." Still, she couldn't quite understand why she was teased and taunted so much. Again she felt that enormous need. "I had this real need to be accepted and loved by people," Halle told the *Cleveland Plain Dealer* in 1999. "The need for love and acceptance drove me into performing."

It also drove her, temporarily, into politics. While in high school, Halle decided to put her popularity to the test. "I was the head cheerleader and president of the class," she said in 2001. "I ran for prom queen and won, but they accused me of stuffing the ballot box. They said we had to flip a coin to determine who the prom queen really was. I picked heads and won again. But that experience stuck with me. I could be president and head cheerleader, but they were white and I was black and I was different. I realized that I always have to keep fighting. . . . They probably hate me now." "I felt like I was accepted there until it came to being prom queen," Halle said in 1996. "It took me a long time to get over it."

In July 2002 I talked to Terrie Fitzwater, one of Halle's former high school classmates. Fitzwater used to work with Halle in the attendance office, which was in the vice principal's office (it was a way of getting out of study hall). It was sometimes boring work—the two of them would sit there, talking about "girl stuff" and waiting for the period to end. Occasionally, they'd actually have to perform their main duty—if a student got in trouble, Terrie or Halle would have to go get them out of class and bring them to the vice principal's office.

Fitzwater recalls that on the day the prom queen vote became known, Halle and another girl were the ones called down to the vice principal's office. The two girls were informed of the tie, but took the news in quite different ways. "Halle was all excited about being prom queen and thought that it would be really cool if there were co-queens," Fitzwater told me. The other girl, however, took another stance—and the atmosphere became charged. "[She] didn't want any part of that, she didn't want to share the title. So that's when they tossed the coin." Fitzwater says the allegations of ballot stuffing were all bogus: "You couldn't really do that because when you went up to vote they had your number and crossed it off after you voted." Bedford High in 1988 was not Florida in 2000.

Halle got some measure of revenge on the night of the prom. She decided she wasn't going to show up. Why should she? How much fun could she really have with people she knew were out to get her, with people who had bared their fangs the first chance they got, with people who didn't value her and didn't trust her? Halle's mother, always the cool head, told her to go. After all, by staying home, she was letting her enemies win. So Halle headed out—fashionably late, haute couture late, half an hour before the prom dinner was set to end anyway. There, at the door of the hall, she saw the entire prom committee standing outside, distraught, wondering what had happened to their queen. Halle smiled— her revenge complete—but she was miserable inside.

Still, it was a controversy that haunted Halle, and her classmates, for years afterward. Halle's Bedford High class was made up of some 450 people, and so there were a lot of folks involved. The controversy was messy and racial, pitting a black girl against a white one, and the whole thing left a lot of kids and parents feeling disturbed. The furor forced many whites in the area to confront issues of race for the first time; Halle, for her part, was still trying to find herself amid all the ugliness around her. Halle said in 2001: "Not everybody would agree that I was smart or funny or had a solid character. 'Pretty' was said about me more than anything else. I got to the point where I loathed hearing it. I loathed being judged by my physical self. Because I knew that was the tiniest part of me. I couldn't take credit for it. I wasn't proud of it. Everyone comes in the package that they come in. I tried really hard to fit in. So I was in every club, the president of my class, in the Honor Society. . . . I never felt equal. I thought if I made the Honor Society they would know I was as smart as they were; if I ran the paper I'd control what's in the paper and make it diverse; if I'm a cheerleader I'm going to be the captain." Despite Halle's memories of alienation, one of her high school classmates, Kelli Hichens, told me "Halle Berry was a very well-liked girl in school. She had friends who were both black and white, and I know many boys would have liked to have dated her regardless of color. It bothers me and my friends that she is now saying that she was racially discriminated against during high school."

Halle learned a hard lesson from the prom queen episode. She told the *New York Times* in 1995: "I had worked hard to be accepted, but when it came to being a standard of beauty for the school, they didn't want me. That taught me. No more dancing bear." Belonging to groups hadn't helped Halle feel like she belonged. Even though she was on the cheerleading squad, one of her classmates told me that the other cheerleaders would always give Halle "a hard time." Was it racial? Nobody can recall exactly what the hazing was about. But being teased by cheerleaders—whatever the reason—isn't a recipe for a happy childhood.

Halle was also dealing with physical changes at the time. "I developed very early," she told the *Daily News* in 1998. "I had boobs when nobody else had them and, believe me, it was not a cool thing to be in the sixth grade being a 34C. I kept telling my mom I wanted to get them taken off. She was saying, 'Hold on honey, one day you'll be sooooo happy.'" Halle has also said in interviews that she struggled with obesity during her late high school years (former classmates, however, say she looked just as pretty as she does now—except for the fact that her hair wasn't as well styled).

While in high school, Halle was not the theatrical type. She never appeared in any Bedford High plays or musicals, but for her senior project she played Tillie, a character from the drama *The Effect of Gamma Rays on Man-in-the-Moon Marigolds*. "She went into this other world," Halle's high school drama teacher, Mary Ann Costa, told the *Washington Post* in 1999. "When you have the ability to create a character that well, you have to tap into something, somehow. Who knows where that came from."

After high school, Halle took a few courses at Cuyahoga Community College. It's a college that draws mostly from the Cleveland community for its student body. Her focus was on the media, but she didn't stick with it long. "I did an internship at a TV station one summer, and they'd send me out on stories, but I couldn't ask people questions," she was quoted as saying in 2000. "I felt it was too intrusive, so I decided journalism wasn't for me."

"I wanted to be a journalist, but I couldn't do it. One of my first assignments, my professor gave me a list of questions that I had to ask an inner-city family whose house had been burned down. I accompanied the lead journalist and had these questions, but I was just bawling. I so lost my composure that it upset the family. I didn't have the skin for the job."

Not long afterward, a boyfriend enrolled her in a beauty contest. Said Halle in 2000: "Beauty can be used as a tool to draw people in. But once you're in, you've got to be able to do something. If you can't, then you're just another pretty face." A new life was just about to open up for Halle.

"Stardom isn't a profession, it's an accident."

—LAUREN BACALL

"I don't like taking no. I fight for roles.
I want the same shot as everyone else."

—HALLE BERRY

TWO

Beauty Queen

It's her first big job. She has always had to work to support herself, she couldn't depend on her mother, who believed in tough love, to bail her out, and she certainly couldn't rely on her daddy, who hardly seemed to believe in love at all, to get her out of jams. It was all on her, always had been since day one when she decided to head out into the world and find herself in show business. Now she had landed a part on a television show, Living Dolls, *a sitcom. But what was this strange feeling coming over her? She lost control of her limbs, couldn't feel her body, and she collapsed. Nobody knew what was wrong. Had the pressure gotten to her? The stress can get to people quick in Hollywood. Had drugs gotten to her? She wouldn't be the first or the last to succumb to narcotics in this town. Was she some sort of showboat, a drama queen, a method actor pulling some attention-getting stunt to make the pages of* Variety *or* USA Today *or* TV Guide? *She wouldn't be the first actress, or the last, to pull some shenanigan to make a splash in the media.*

Medical assistance was called. Doctors were consulted. It wasn't stress, it wasn't drugs, it wasn't a public relations ploy. She didn't know what was wrong. But she was about to find out.

It was never easy. I remember talking to Halle Berry's mother in 1992 and asking her what it was like raising two young daughters on her own. "I was a single mom," Judith Berry told me. "It was tough, money-wise, when she was growing up. There wasn't money for things like movies." Young Halle used to get her film fix from watching old flicks on TV. She would watch *The Wizard of Oz* and reenact the entire film, imitating Dororthy's part and even Toto's. Like Dorothy, the Tin Man, the Cowardly Lion, and the Scarecrow, Halle needed things: courage to face her fears, wisdom to find the right career, and emotional control to handle all the strange barbed feelings that were welling up in her heart. Her mother was there but could only guide her to the start of her journey. Her father was estranged and his sister was a stranger. There was no Yellow Brick Road. Halle would not only have to find her way on her own, she'd also have to clear her own path.

So Halle headed out on her own road. In the beginning it wasn't about fame, it wasn't even about learning the craft of entertainment. When Halle was in high school, she gave little thought to the idea of becoming an actress. In the past, she has been very up front about what set her on her journey: It was money. Halle told Barbara Walters in 2002: "I wanted to make a lot of money. . . . Just to really better the quality of life for my family. Especially my mother ... Not to be famous ... Never to be an actress ... I thought, what can I do that'll make a lot of money so that one day I can buy my mother a house? You know, a big fancy house. That's what I wanted to do for my mother."

It was also about luck. In 1983, when Halle Berry was seventeen, her first serious boyfriend secretly sent off two pictures of her to a statewide beauty contest. Halle realized then that she could use her looks to make money to get out of Cleveland and go on to bigger and better things. Halle told the *Bay State Banner* in 1993: "I got into pageants to win scholarship money. We were very middle-class people. Not upper middle. Not lower middle. Just middle. And I knew that my mother couldn't afford to flat-out send me or my sister to college. So my only hope was through scholarships and grants."

Halle moved from Cleveland to Chicago, hoping to pursue opportunities in entertainment. Her first few weeks there were like something out of the Stevie Wonder song "Living for the City": Halle got back from a job in Milwaukee only to find that her roommate had skipped out early, leaving Halle to pay the $1,300 rent bill on her own. Halle turned to her mother to help bail her out, but Judith gave her tough love in return and refused to lend her the cash. If Halle wanted to live out her dreams in the big city, she was going to have to figure out how to finance them on her own.

"Mom, I really need, like, fifty dollars for food," Halle pleaded.

"You wanted to go there. Now you're seeing what it's like in the real world," her mother answered.

The two did not speak for almost a whole year afterward. But Halle did get something out of the confrontation, even if it wasn't something she could fold and put in her pocketbook: "She made me realize I had to either sink or swim," Halle said to *People* in 1996. "From that moment on I became independent." Halle also learned how to live on the cheap. She would take the bus every day because she didn't have a car, enduring all the pick-up lines and come-ons from the men who would hit on her. She also started to hang out at bars that offered patrons free munchies. Said Halle: "Me and my model friends hung out at a lot of happy hours eating [free] drumsticks."

It was ironic that a woman seeking to escape the confines of skin color and appearance would turn to the pageant circuit to find what she was looking for. Beauty pageants are by definition skin-deep affairs: The plastic hosts. The saline chests. The big hair. The bigger expectations. The high heels. The low necklines. The stiff walks across the stage. The artificial smiles across the faces. The fronting. The backstabbing. The "talent" competition. The "celebrity" judges. The sashes. The swimsuits. The Q and A. The T and A. The rehearsals. The dance numbers. The cameras. The commercial breaks. The runners-up. The running down. The tiaras. The group hugs. The one big winner. The forty-nine small losers. But, in the end, Halle said her pageant experience was a positive one. "You're exploited if you allow yourself to be," she told *People* in 1993. "Only good things came out of my pageant days."

One thing Halle learned from the beauty pageant circuit was how to handle victory and defeat. Backstage at the contests, she saw more than her fair share of bad winners and bad losers. She told *Playboy* in 1994: "After the pageant, the bad loser will go around bad-mouthing everything. She'll put down the girl who won 'Look at her—she has fake tits! She has acne!' Just being obnoxious. She can't get over the fact that she lost: 'Hello? You didn't win, go home now.'"

"A bad winner? I knew this after judging pageants. During the interviews these girls give their perfect pageant answers: 'Yes, I'd like to save the world.' Then afterward at the dinner with the winners, these girls turn into total snobs. They've already used you and abused you and gotten what they wanted out of you—the crown. Then they're like monsters."

In grade school, Halle had been uneasy with her looks. When she attended an all-black school in inner-city Cleveland, black girls taunted her, teased her, and sometimes attacked her. Fellow students would comment on her light brown skin, her dark brown eyes, and want to touch—and sometimes tug—her dark brown hair. When she moved to a mostly white school in the suburbs, white girls teased her, taunted her, and sometimes jumped her—and her new classmates were similarly fascinated by, and sometimes repelled by, her complexion and her hair texture and color. Halle was also uncomfortable with her curves; they attracted the stares of boys and the ire of girls, she didn't quite know what to do with her sexuality, she hadn't quite figured out how to bottle it, how to contain it. But after some time in the pageant circuit, things started to make sense. She could finally look in the mirror and realize that she was seeing something special—after all, she had the tiara to prove it. Said Halle in 1993: "Through my pageant experience I became very secure with myself and my body. I learned how to take care of myself and to deal with people. I started taking acting classes and then I moved to New York. Although I knew modeling wasn't something I could do forever, it was good money and gave me a chance to travel. It was a means to an end, even though at the time I wasn't sure what that end might be."

So, as she once said, she spent a lot of time with a crown on her head. In 1984 she won the Miss Teen All-America Pageant. In 1986 she was first runner-up at the Miss USA pageant, and later that year won the dress competition in the Miss World Pageant, where she finished third overall. In 2002 I talked to Syd Friedman, a Fairview Park pageant producer and theatrical agent who had seen Halle on the pageant circuit in the 1980s. Friedman told me what he thought was the secret to Halle's success: "I think she had a personality. It was not only her prettiness—she bubbled over in her personality. She was a real sweet girl and she could make an awful lot of contact with the various judges with it. She bubbled over. She was one of the girls I would have selected as having the potential to go on to bigger and better things. She sells herself with a lot of enthusiasm." Around that time Halle attended a reception in Pittsburgh, Pennsylvania. People who saw her then were struck by her blend of grace and beauty—and her lack of pretension. She was a beautiful woman, yes; she seemed to be aware of her effect on other people, of course; but despite all that, she was easy to talk to, quick to laugh, and comfortable around crowds and strangers.

Halle said in 2001: "It was very shallow in many ways, because it perpetuated my physical self a lot more than I ever wanted to, but very significant in a way because I gained a lot of confidence in myself. That confidence has served me throughout my life. . . . In my case, I believe it was good for the pageant system for someone of color to win. They were taking too much heat that there were too many black contestants and none of them were even placing. They couldn't deny us any longer. So, did I win for real, or was I the black girl who won to make a statement? I don't know. . . . To win something like that made me feel accepted. As shallow or superficial as it may have been, in that moment I felt like I am as good as they are."

In subsequent years, after Halle had hung up her tiara, she would laugh off her experiences as a beauty queen and as a model. Said Halle in 2002 to *Movieline*: "I did it for three years. I hated it, it was the most boring work I ever did. There had to be a better way to make a buck! [Laughs] Not being able to have a say. Being a human coat hanger." But there was one thing she learned from that period in her life. "Pageants teach you how to lose and not be devastated," Halle told the *New York Times* in 1995. "It was great preparation for Hollywood."

Halle wasn't the first model to become an actress, and she won't be the last. Of course, the whole idea of models wanting to be actors is something of a bad joke; all models seem to want to become thespians, just as all actors seem eventually to want to direct. People remember all the models who didn't make it as actors: Cindy Crawford, who appeared in the ludicrous thriller *Fair Game;* Naomi Campbell, who appeared in the best-forgotten *Cool as Ice* opposite rapper/actor wanna-be Vanilla Ice. But a number of models, like Halle, actually have made it big in Hollywood, but after they become successful, they typically stop talking about their model pasts, as if it were some sort of twisted family secret. Lauren Bacall was hired by Howard Hawks after he saw her in a layout in *Harper's Bazaar.* Peter Bogdanovich saw Cybill Shepherd on the cover of *Glamour* magazine and cast her as the lead in his movie *The Last Picture Show.* Jessica Lange, Sharon Stone, Kim Basinger, and Rene Russo have three things in common: (1) they're all fine actresses, (2) they're all former models, and (3) they'd all prefer that you only knew about number 1.

Although some models have made it as actresses, the fact is most wash out. Modeling and acting are not interchangeable professions. Models tend to have stiff faces and inert demeanors—they can "vogue" and strike a pose, they can cop some attitude, they can fill out clothes, but there's a big difference between doing those things and playing a lead role in *Long Day's Journey into Night.* Actors, good ones anyway, tend to have mobile faces, with lots of lines and facial muscles that move and eyes surrounded by lines and creases that can hold emotions. Study Robert De Niro's face, or Denzel Washington's; look closely at Meryl Streep or Angela Bassett. In order to play a character it helps if one's face has character.

Another myth: Actors are all good-looking. Actually, many actors are rather odd-looking. They have extreme features that can be on the grotesque side. Partly, it's their strange looks that propelled them into acting—so they could wear costumes, put on makeup, speak other people's words, and literally become other people. Through the strength of their acting, and the power of their fame, they become beautiful. Their extreme features, like masks in Greek tragedies or costumes on Halloween, arrest our attention, capture our fascination, and help make them stars. Barbra Streisand is a good example of an arresting-looking actress with features that might be considered extreme by the mainstream (personally, I think she's beautiful), but there are others: Humphrey Bogart's droopy brow; Will Smith's big ears; Tom Cruise's nose; Meryl Streep's nose; Betty Davis's swimming pool eyes; Jennifer Lopez's roomy, much-talked about behind; James Woods's pockmarked cheeks; Jack Nicholson's wolfish grin.

We are attracted by the extreme; we go to movies to be taken out of our lives and immersed in the extraordinary. Certainly many, if not most, movie stars are exceeding beautiful/handsome, by any standard: Sanaa Lathan, Natalie Portman, Taye Diggs, Salma Hayek, Brad Pitt, Nicole Kidman, and Gong Li to name a few. But there are other stars who make us believe in the fantasy of their beauty, and it is these stars that fascinate. Tom Hanks is not a great-looking guy—but he is arguably the world's biggest star. Judi Dench is not a raving beauty, but through her craft she can generate a kind of radiance.

Halle Berry, of course, is stunning, no two ways about it. She's as lovely in person as she is on the movie screen. She's short of stature, but she exudes a sweetness that can fill a room like a bouquet of freshly picked flowers. There's a kind of glow that people get after they've spent some time in the sun, or after they've exercised, or in the wake of a peak experience, like being kissed on the cheek for the first time. It goes beyond sweat, or mere blushing—it's a sort of emotional radiance. Halle seems to have that glow all the time, regardless of whether she's been to the beach, exercised, or been kissed. But society didn't always rate her as a beauty; her classmates didn't always appreciate her looks, modeling agencies and beauty pageant judges and casting agents often devalued her and sometimes she even sold herself short. Through force of will and the changing fashions of the times, Halle turned her visage, her form, her skin tone and hair texture into a standard of beauty. She now carries with her a kind of cultural force, the energy of the outside turned inside, of the forbidden made acceptable, that never would have come together had she been a white, blue-eyed blonde from Los Angeles.

"Beauty is not just physical," Halle told *Ebony* in August 2000. "It's about what you stand for, how you live your life." She told *Jet* in 1992 that she was proud of her accomplishment: "To have blacks and whites view you as a sex symbol, when there's Marilyn Monroe and Kim Basinger, it lets the world know black women can be sex symbols too."

But being a sex object wasn't enough for Halle. She wanted to be an actress. She signed up with a manager, Vincent Cirrincione, who began to send her out on auditions. Said Cirrincione in 1996: "I sent her out for a NYNEX commercial, and she showed up having cut off all her long hair. I looked at that short crop and said, 'Well, there goes your commercial career.' And she said, 'That's not why I'm here.'"

She wanted the big time, and she decided the small screen was the place to go first. There were setbacks. She auditioned for *Days of Our Lives* but failed to get a role. She auditioned for a revamped version of Charlie's Angels—not so cleverly titled *Charlie's Angels 88*—and again failed to nab a part. Being a model, it turned out, hurt her chances more than enhanced them. Said Halle to the *Los Angeles Times* in 1995: "When you're a model, they think you're stupid and they think, 'Oh you're beautiful, so you want to be in movies, but you have no talent.'" But she tried to turn her looks into an advantage. As she told the *Orange County Register* in 1993:

"Beauty can be used as a tool to draw people in. But once you're in, you've got to be able to do something. If you can't, then you're just another pretty face. . . . I don't think I'm bad-looking, and I know my looks have made a difference in some situations. I know that element is there, but I also see a lot of people around me who are much more beautiful than I am."

Halle had received more than her fair share of attacks for her looks, but she had also received, as one might imagine, any number of compliments, some appreciated, some unwanted. She had come to believe, however, that in some strange way, compliments and insults looped back into one another, actually became one another. People who made fun of her looks were clearly insecure, threatened—and in a way were complimenting her because they were saying that her attractiveness was intense enough to cause them to lash out. But people who praised her looks were, in another way, also insulting her—after all, she had other things to offer beyond her apple cheeks, her chest, her butt, and her legs. By focusing on her looks they were ignoring the rest of her, reducing her to what could be seen and felt and kissed and stroked. She was more than that. Halle told the *Washington Post* in 1999 that for a long time "everybody tried to make believe that [my beauty] was the best thing about me. Then I realized no, that's not the best thing about me, that could all be taken away tomorrow and I'd still have all the gifts that I have on the inside."

And so she fought. She had learned how to fight as a kid growing up. She had seen her mother fight her father, seen her sister fight her father; Halle herself had had her battles with white kids and black kids. She was a veteran of conflict; after the wars she had been through, casting agents and directors were nothing. "I don't like taking no," Halle said in 1995. "I fight for roles. I want the same shot as everyone else." Halle's manager was also a pugilist when it came to getting his client good work. Halle told the *New York Times* in 2002: "Vince is a bull-dog. Neither one of us knew what we were doing, but we went ahead anyway. He won't take no for an answer. He'll try every angle to get me into the room to be seen. That's what he says. 'I'll get you into the room and then you do your thing.' And getting in the room, especially if you're a black actor, is the hardest part."

The fighting paid off. In 1989 she landed her first big role: the part of Emily Franklin in the ABC sitcom *Living Dolls*. The success came from rejection: Though she was turned down for a part on *Charlie's Angels 88*, she nonetheless caught the eye of Aaron Spelling, the producer behind such hits as *Mod Squad, Dynasty, Beverly Hills 90210,* and *Melrose Place.* Halle told the *Atlanta Journal-Constitution* in 1994: "It was what happened at that audition that made me consider acting."

Living Dolls was only on the air for a few weeks. It was one of those sitcoms that probably sounded great when it was pitched: a comedy about young models! It was nearly unwatchable when it hit the small screen. Shows get launched based on good pitches—where a writer or producers spends fifteen minutes explaining his concept. As a result, shows that are shallow, and thus easier to pitch, make it on the air. Shows that have depth and complexity, and which are therefore harder to pitch, get rejected. (Imagine, say, trying to pitch *Hamlet* to the networks. "It's about this guy named Hamlet whose father is killed." "What does he do about it?" "He stages a play within a play and thinks about committing suicide." "Is there a love interest?" "Yeah, but she dies." "Who kills her?" "She commits suicide." "Does everyone in this play die?" "Well, yeah, at the end, pretty much.")

All you really need to know about *Living Dolls* is this: It was a spin-off of the Tony Danza sitcom *Who's the Boss*. (Hollywood Rule No. 178. Never appear in anything that's a spin-off of something Tony Danza once did.) *Living Dolls* starred Leah Remini (who would later find some fame on CBS's *The King of Queens*) as Charlie, a tough street kid turned model living in a house with other aspiring models. All the women fit into neat little character boxes: Deborah Tucker played the bratty model, Alison Elliot was the innocent model, and Halle Berry was the smart model who wanted to go to medical school. It was pasted by the critics. Howard Rosenberg of the *Los Angeles Times* wrote: *"Living Dolls* is bad enough when it tries to be funny, even worse when it tries not to be funny. As for the latter, it doesn't have to try." Ray Richmond wrote in the *Orange County Register*: "The sitcom-by-numbers writing is numbingly bad, the acting horrendous, the pacing terrible. And those are the good points."

The reviews turned out to be the least of Halle's worries at the time. She was filming an episode of *Living*

Dolls when she suddenly and unexpectedly collapsed on the set. She was taken to the hospital and a battery of tests was run. Halle was scared and confused. The doctors were saying things to her and she was translating them in her head into disaster. Physicians told her "you have diabetes" and she heard "you're dying of cancer." She didn't know exactly what diabetes was. All she knew was that she was twenty-two years old and she was just starting her career and she had passed out and she was sick with an ailment she didn't understand and this sort of thing just wasn't supposed to happen to someone who was twenty-two years old and just starting her career. "All I heard was shots every day and that I could lose my eyesight and my legs," Halle told *Ladies' Home Journal* in 1997. "I was scared to death." Another worry: Halle was in a pressure-filled profession; diabetes is an ailment that becomes more dangerous in such conditions. Halle told the *Atlanta Journal-Constitution* in 1994: "Sometimes my blood sugar goes really high and I get really sick." She told *Ebony* in 1995: "Stress has a lot to do with diabetes and there is a lot of it in this business."

Diabetes occurs when the body can't produce or respond to insulin, which is a hormone that allows blood sugar (glucose) to pass into the cells of the body and thus generate energy. Warning signs include frequent urination, tingling in fingers and toes, nausea, fatigue, vomiting, and excessive thirst. Diabetes comes in two forms: insulin-dependent or Type I, and non-insulin-dependent Type 2. There are an estimated sixteen million people in the United States who have diabetes. About one in three people who have the disease are undiagnosed, so there are about six million people who have diabetes but don't know it—yet. African Americans are significantly more at risk to develop diabetes—more than two million African Americans, or one in ten, have the disease. Diabetes is the leading cause of heart attacks, strokes, blindness, kidney failure, and amputations. Complications from diabetes kill more people than AIDS and breast cancer—combined. The death rate for diabetes is 27 percent higher for blacks than it is for whites.

Obesity is a main contributing risk factor to diabetes, so as Americans get fatter and eat more junk food, the diabetes rate has skyrocketed. The Centers for Disease Control predicted in 2002 that the rate of diabetes will soar 165 percent over the next fifty years unless Americans make some major lifestyle changes. Because African Americans tend to eat a lot of fried fatty foods, it opens that population up to diabetes.

Halle, at first, didn't want to believe the diagnosis. She didn't want to face an insulin needle three times a day. She didn't want to change her life: her eating habits, her exercise habits, her emotional outlook. So she did nothing for a long time. It wasn't until a few years later when she (temporarily) lost the use of her right leg because of the diabetes that she finally made some lifestyle changes—cutting sweets and fried foods out of her diet, hiring a personal trainer. She was scared of the needles she needed in order to inject herself with insulin, but she came to terms with the fact that she either faced the needles or died. She also came to the conclusion that, of all the ailments she could get, she was in some ways lucky that she got one that was manageable—after all, you can't always "manage" cancer.

Her career in showbiz seemed over before it had really begun. After *Living Dolls* was canceled in 1989, Halle didn't work for six months. Critics had panned the show. She was sick with a life-threatening ailment she didn't fully understand. Her parents and her only sister weren't there to help her out. And she didn't know exactly what she was going to do next. "When you go through bad times," Halle told the *Plain Dealer* in 1999, "you find where your great capacity to learn is. And I've been through really bad times with my career and personal life. Behind all that are lessons that can make you stronger."

A five-foot, five-inch guy named Spike was about to give her lessons in toughness.

"Hollywood is a place where they'll
pay you a thousand dollars for a kiss
and fifty cents for your soul."
                    —MARILYN MONROE

"When I first got here, no one thought I
could walk and talk at the same time."
                    —HALLE BERRY

THREE

Revolution in Black

She was supposed to be the wife. That's why Spike Lee had called her in. She had a sweet face, with cheeks as round as cooking apples and a smile like a mouthful of stars. She had middle-class values written all over her—no, it was engraved on her, in the same fancy lettering people use on wedding invitations and birth announcements. But she didn't want to play the wife. There was another role she had her eye on—the tough-talking crackhead. She wanted to challenge her image, not play into it. She wanted to go beyond what she knew. It was a small part, but a striking one, something an actress could really sink her teeth into, something that would grab a viewer's attention. If she played this part, and played it well, people would never think of her as just another pretty face. Then again, if she failed, she would fail spectacularly, and the whole world would know the limits of her talent. But it was worth the risk; she wanted that role and she pressed for it. The director didn't think she was right for the crackhead role, didn't think she could play it, but if she wanted to give it a go, they'd let her read. She was satisfied. That's all she wanted really. A chance. Now she had one. She would make the best of it.

"I am invisible, understand, simply because people refuse to see me." Ralph Ellison wrote that line near the start of *Invisible Man,* his classic novel about American life. For him, black people were invisible to whites. Oh, they could hear black people just fine—they listened to blues, and called it folk; they heard R and B and called it rock; and, after the Age of Ellison, they grooved to the beat of hip-hop and called it Vanilla Ice and the Beastie Boys and Eminem. But in 1986, White America finally saw Black America when director Spike Lee released the film called *She's Gotta Have It.* Blacks had been making films before, of course. Oscar Micheaux started up his Oscar Micheaux Corporation in 1918, churning out short features to begin with and then going on to put out full-length films. In 1973, during the blaxploitation film era, a time of big Afros, loud clothes, and black-power-to-the-people rhetoric, Melvin Van Peebles wrote, directed, and starred in the gritty, violent film *Sweet Sweetback's Badasssss Song.* But Spike Lee's project, made for $175,000 and ultimately grossing more than $7 million, inspired a new generation of black filmmakers to pick up cameras and make their own movies. Lee published books about filmmaking and demystified the process; he didn't make action films or exploitation films, he made commercial art films that explored social themes with fire and wit; he wasn't giving audiences only what they wanted, he was giving them what he thought they needed. Early on, Halle Berry was swept up in the black film revolution that Lee helped launch.

In the wake of the success of *She's Gotta Have It,* a number of other films directed by African Americans were released. There was the comedy *Hollywood Shuffle* (1987), a satirical take on making it in Tinseltown starring and directed by Robert Townsend. There was *I'm Gonna Git You Sucka* (1988), a send-up of blaxploitation films starring and directed by Keenen Ivory Wayans. There was *Boyz N the Hood* (1991), a gritty coming-of-age tale set in South Central Los Angeles directed by John Singleton. And, later, there was another tale of gangs and violence titled *Menace II Society* (1993), directed by the Hughes Brothers.

Black films created Halle Berry. She was not a creation of Hollywood; she was not a protégée of a white director or star. Spike Lee discovered her when he cast her in *Jungle Fever.* Then Kevin Hooks, another black filmmaker, launched her when he directed her in his film *Strictly Business.* And the Hudlin Brothers made her a star when they cast her opposite Eddie Murphy in their upscale comedy *Boomerang.* Without black filmmakers, Halle wouldn't have happened.

Hollywood has misused and ignored African-American female talent in the past—Lena Horne, Diana Ross, Dorothy Dandridge, and others had fought, unsuccessfully, to get solid, mainstream roles, and found them few and far between. Those rare times when Hollywood did confer stardom on a black actress (or some flimsy thing resembling stardom), it was often granted in a form so malignant, so repulsive that it was rejected by the majority of black people. In 1954, after Eartha Kitt had broken out to become a minor sex symbol in Hollywood, *Ebony* magazine, which almost never ran critical articles of black celebrities, was so taken aback by the cold, carnal image that had been created for her that it ran a cover story entitled "Why Negroes Do Not Like Eartha Kitt." Halle was fortunate to come of age in an era when, for the first time in Hollywood history, there was a support structure of black filmmakers looking to make nonexploitative films about the black experience.

As a result of the black film revolution of the late eighties and nineties there were more spots available for people of color in front of and behind the camera than ever before. Previously, the Hollywood lie had been: "Mainstream America didn't want to hear black stories—and therefore films starring black people weren't profitable enough to get made." But the fact is, around the 1980s, black musical culture was all the rage. Hip-hop artists from rap godfathers Run-DMC to gangsta rappers such as Snoop Doggy Dogg to Dr. Dre were starting to dominate the charts and to command the attention and wallets of American kids, black and white. Clearly America wanted to hear about black life. It only made sense that they wanted to see it as well. When Lee's film proved black film could be profitable and popular, a number of other black filmmakers were able to grab their shots as well. Hollywood didn't open the floodgates, but at least a trickle had started.

I had the opportunity to interview Spike Lee several times around this period, chatting with him around the release of *Do the Right Thing* (1989), *Mo' Better Blues* (1990), and *Jungle Fever* (1991). Driving around with him in Manhattan (or being driven, Spike, a child of the subways, doesn't know how to drive) one could feel the respect and love New Yorkers, particularly nonwhite ethnic New Yorkers, had for the maverick director. People would try to hand him scripts, business cards, baked goods. Crowds would gather wherever he was. His offices were located in Brooklyn at the time, right in his home base in Bed-Stuy, so there was a sense that he was walking it like he was talking it; he portrayed himself as a race man, a community guy, and here he was, working in the neighborhood, filming in the neighborhood, and employing casts and crews that were predominantly black.

Originally, Lee considered Halle for the part of his wife in the film. It was a comfortable, middle-class part—a school teacher's spouse—that was eventually played by another model-turned-actress, Veronica Webb. Lee didn't think Halle looked right for the showier role as a crackhead—she was too pretty, too gentle, too nice, but she asked for the chance to audition and won the role. "Frankly, fighting against my looks has become a large part of my career as an actress," Halle told the *New York Times* in December 23, 2001. "I mean, everyone should have such problems, but producers never consider me for anything that isn't glamorous."

The part was more than just another role for Halle; it

was an announcement that she was not afraid to do the dirty work that great acting required. "I wanted, in a major way, to make a statement," Halle told *The Observer* in August 2000. "To come out swinging and hopefully have people see me for something other than what was on my résumé at the time, which was modeling."

So now Halle had what she wanted—a showy role playing a Harlem crackhead. There were only two problems: first, she didn't know much about Harlem, and second, she didn't know anything about crackheads. Luckily, Samuel L. Jackson, who played Gator, Halle's addict boyfriend in the movie, was willing to help. In the movie, Vivian, the crackhead played by Halle, and Gator, find themselves on the move to support their habits—at one point we see them in a huge crackhouse nicknamed "the Taj Mahal." To prepare for the role, Jackson took Halle around New York City to various drug-infested neighborhoods so they could get a feel for the kind of places their characters were living in. Jackson recognized Halle's talent early and wanted to help her make the best of it. The trip helped inspire Halle. She didn't bathe for several days, immersing herself in the part. She found that, buried deep inside, there was a part of her that wanted to try cocaine, wanted to see what the fuss was all about, what the thrill actually entailed. But she never gave in to it. She couldn't imagine putting anything in her nose—it seemed like it would hurt. She stayed focused on her acting. Jackson liked what he saw and has remained fond of her ever since. "When you look at Halle, you think ingenue,"

Samuel L. Jackson told the *New York Times* in 2002. "I told her, 'This is the kind of role that will take that curse off you forever.'"

Halle's relationship with Lee wasn't as smooth. Lee had very strong views on interracial relationships that weren't shared by other members of the cast, including co-star Annabella Sciorra (who plays a white temp who falls for a black architect) and Halle. Halle once said: "I remember having a big row with Spike Lee on the set of *Jungle Fever* because he said my parents divorced because black/white love can never work. I told Spike that that was just his warped and twisted point of view. The reality was that my parents loved each other and when I was conceived it was done with love and then they split up because of my father's drinking."

Halle admired Lee, but to a point—and basically that point was the tip of his tongue. She didn't like some of the things he said, and the way some of the things he said, the sociopolitical things, matched up to what he did. She thought he had a one-track mind, for one, and that he was entirely focused on his own personal views. She thought he'd be better off directing films that he didn't write, just to get him out of his own head. Halle also resented the fact that Lee was so focused, in his public commentary, on being pro-black, and yet, in her view, he tended to date light, almost white-looking black women. She thought it was surprising at best, hypocritical at worst. She thought his point of view on such matters was narrow and isolated, and that his idea of beauty was very limited.

There has been lots of speculation over the years as to whether Halle and Spike actually dated. She has denied it. She says she showed up to work on *Jungle Fever* radiating a "don't hit on me" vibe. She has added that she thinks Spike picked up on it, because, according to her, no attempt was made. Still, it's interesting to note that during the filming of *Jungle Fever,* Halle lived in a room above Spike's Joint, a store that Lee ran in Brooklyn to sell film memorabilia and merchandise.

When *Jungle Fever* was released in 1991, I talked to Sciorra about the film and some of the tensions on the set. Lee, apparently, had the opinion that interracial relationships—at least the one depicted in the film—were fueled by the stereotypes that the two lovers involved had about race. Sciorra believed that her character was truly motivated by love and played her role that way. "There were differences in the way we both viewed the initial attraction from one character to another," Sciorra told me in 1991 in an interview for *USA Today.* "But it wasn't a great difference." I got the sense, however, that some of the racial tensions that were depicted in *Jungle Fever* spilled, to a certain degree, onto the set in real life.

One of the most interesting things about *Jungle Fever* is that it's not really about what it's about. It bills itself as a film about the social, emotional, and sometimes physical perils of interracial romance. Angela (Sciorra) a working-class Italian temp from the white enclave of Bensonhurst falls in love, or at least lust, with an upper-middle-class black architect from Harlem named

Flipper (Wesley Snipes). There's a nice sequence, played out over a series of late-night meals, where Angela and Flipper talk about some of the stereotypes that rule and divide them—and then the pair, shorn of their prejudices, shed their clothes as well, and make love right in the office, right on Flipper's desk.

But the real story is the subplot in which Gator (who happens to be Flipper's brother) and Vivian tear apart Flipper's family structure and neighborhood. In the first scene in which she appears, Halle's performance as Vivian is striking—she is seen at Gator's side on an outdoor basketball court late at night. Her eyes are wide as if she is permanently startled; her movements are quick and jerky, as if she expects attackers to leap out from the shadows. Her clothes are tattered and her skin is blemished. She and Gator immediately launch into an obscenity-laced drug-fueled argument that proceeds at a hundred miles an hour. It is an argument nearly incomprehensible to outsiders—the indecipherability of their words seems to suggest that they are a matched pair of doomed souls, their utterances, lives, and choices intelligible only to each other.

Jungle Fever, in the end, is about misdirection. How idiotic it is, the film seems to say, for people to be focusing on issues like interracial sex when there are real problems to be discussed. Interracial sex never hurt anybody, but everyone's worked up about it. Meanwhile drugs are polluting residential streets and tearing homes apart. In one scene, John Turturro, who plays a lovelorn Italian shopkeeper, assails some of his regulars for complaining constantly about blacks and then not even bothering to vote. At the climax of the film, in a sequence of startling power, Gator robs his parents— "Mama, I smoked the TV," he says at one point—and, mocking his father, performs a demonic, insolent dance. In another scene, Vivian—her hair wild, her blouse fallen open—crudely offers to perform a sexual act on Flipper for five dollars and then, when he refuses (he's walking his young daughter to school), she drops her rate down to three dollars. It's a tribute to Halle's immersion in the character that a tryst with her, in the context of the film, seems utterly foul.

Halle has another fine scene later in the film when Flip goes looking for his brother Gator, who has gone missing. He finds both Gator and Vivian smoking crack on a propped up mattress in the Taj Mahal. He leaves in disgust, and as Stevie Wonder's ode to urban problems "Living for the City" plays on the sound track, we see Vivian and Gator interact. Gator is lost in thought— moved, it seems, by the fact that he has finally alienated his brother for good. Vivian, cursing him, takes a hit of crack; then, sharing her bounty, she forces the pipe into Gator's mouth and then slaps him and takes it back. All of this plays out almost wordlessly—it is a mating dance of shared addiction, shared pain, and shared loneliness. Halle has never looked worse and rarely shined brighter.

Jungle Fever was a solid hit, especially in relation to its modest budget of $14 million. Its domestic box office was $32,482,000.

In the press, Spike is often portrayed as a troublemaker,

a guy who likes to stir things up just for the sake of stirring things up, a guy who is all talk and no substance. In fact, Lee is one of the great career builders in Hollywood and he's launched more talent than perhaps any other director. He doesn't just talk a good game about empowering African Americans in film, he's backed it up by discovering a dizzying array of fresh talent:

- Pre-Spike, Larry Fishburne had a bit part in *Apocalypse Now* and a recurring role as a Cowboy on CBS's *Pee-wee's Playhouse*. After co-starring in Lee's *School Daze* he became a star, with such movies as *Boyz N the Hood, What's Love Got to Do With It,* and *The Matrix*.
- Pre-Spike, Martin Lawrence was just another stand-up comic. After appearing in *Do the Right Thing,* he became one of the hottest stand-ups around and also starred in a number of big-budget movies, including *Bad Boys*.
- Pre-Spike, John Turturro was a marginal actor. After co-starring in *Do the Right Thing* as a bigoted Italian pizza shop worker, he went on to win the Palm d'Or at Cannes for the Coen Brothers film *Barton Fink*.
- Pre-Spike, Denzel Washington had never had a romantic leading man role; after appearing in Lee's *Mo' Better Blues* he went on to star in Lee's *Malcolm X,* following that up with *Crimson Tide* and, of course, he later delivered an Oscar-winning performance in the movie *Training Day*.

- A number of other actors, including Mekhi Phifer (who debuted in Lee's *Clockers* [1995] and went on to star in TV's *ER*), also had their careers kick-started by Lee.

But there's a flipside: With so many minority actors—from Wesley Snipes to Giancarlo Esposito—getting a break from Lee and going on to have significant, sometimes Oscar-winning careers, one has to wonder how much talent was lost in past decades. Until the mid-eighties, Hollywood paid little attention to black actors and filmmakers, and so there were few opportunities for minority actors to prove their worth. Billy Dee Williams, who appeared, memorably, in *Mahogany* and *Lady Sings the Blues* in the seventies and *The Empire Strikes Back* and *Return of the Jedi* in the eighties, complained in 2002 that Hollywood never really gave him a chance to take on substantial roles after that quartet of films. One has to wonder how many other Billy Dee Williamses were never even heard from, or how many other Halle Berrys or Laurence Fishburnes never even got a shot in the twenties, thirties, forties, fifties, sixties, seventies, and early eighties.

In 1991, Halle was able to build on her career with a part in the comedy *Strictly Business*. When I interviewed her for *USA Today* in 1991 about her role in that movie, she was not only excited about that part, she was excited about all the possibilities in front of her: She was meeting people, reading for roles, getting around Hollywood, even writing her own spec scripts. Like many other

African Americans in the film industry, she had been inspired by Spike Lee and wanted to have an impact. Black filmmakers and actors had beaten the door down and now they were trying to take advantage of any opportunities they could. "Black women need to put their energy into their own projects," Halle told me then. "Like Spike Lee, someone has got to be a pioneer and get it done, keep trying when doors are slammed in your face."

In July 2002, I talked to Kevin Hooks, the director of *Strictly Business*, about working with Halle. He told me: "I actually had met Halle on a movie I did about two years earlier called *Heatwave* on TNT. Halle came in to read for the [part of the] girlfriend of Blair Underwood, who was the lead on that film. That was the first time I met her. I was struck by a number of things. First of all she was gorgeous. She was among a group of other actresses in the hallway and she was the one closest to my office door. When I looked outside my office door I saw this woman sitting there and she was just stunning. And I realized she was there to read for that role. We spoke. She wound up not getting that role, but you could tell that this was a girl who was very self-assured and self-confident and very humble and sweet. Someone that you just felt you wanted to see do well. You meet so many people that have an angle who are cynical and manipulative. That's what Hollywood tends to be about. She's really an exception to that."

When Hooks finally worked with Halle on *Strictly Business*, he got a chance to see her honing her acting craft at a very early stage of her career, and he was impressed. Hooks told me: "*Strictly Business* being a comedy was not consistent with the kind of work she honed later in her career. Technique in a comedy is really about finding the moment and trying to make the best of it, finding the most spontaneous moment that you can." Because *Strictly Business* was low-budget, Hooks had to work fast—and Halle helped energize the production by showing an inquisitive spirit. Hooks said to me: "I had about a day or two of rehearsals. Halle had the most questions of anybody there. She made it clear that she was the type of actress who really wanted to absorb as much about the character as she possibly could going into it, so she could then sort of wear the character, so to speak, during the filming of it. I remember her trying to get as much information as she possibly could to bank—almost as if she was putting it all onto a computer hard drive, so she could recall it when the moment felt right. That was the most impressive thing I saw with her at the time."

Although Halle was methodical in her preparation, her performance was unselfconscious. Hooks said to me: "Working with her during the film itself, she seemed to be very spontaneous. She was somewhat of a chameleon in different scenes and situations. She was able to go with the flow and explore different options on the spot. Those kinds of actors are always much more fun and creative to collaborate with. So she even was, at that time, with this comedy, preparing herself for those kinds of relationships in her film career."

Strictly Business, on the surface, seems slight, but, like any really good film comedy, upon closer examination it reveals itself to be intelligently constructed. Laughter requires something to laugh at, so a comedic film has to set a foundation; comedy requires timing and finesse, and so a comedic film has to set up its laughs with care.

African-American comedies have it even harder: It's hard to make a black comedy without selling out. The whole history of African Americans on film is shot through with performers catering to white expectations and stereotypes in order to get a laugh, or catering to self-loathing among some black patrons. Because comedy often requires that foundation of understanding in order to get a laugh (Nixon is a crook, Clinton slept around, Michael Jackson is weird), it's easy to fall back on stereotypes to get a crowd reaction. It's far tougher to do what really good comedians like Chris Rock, Woody Allen, and Janeane Garofalo do—create a whole new way of looking at the world by means of a joke. For the *Our Gang* shorts of the 1920s, movie executives literally transformed a young black child, one Allen Clayton Hoskins Jr., into the stereotypical images in their brains, renaming the actor Farina (evoking the image of hot cereal), giving him pickaninny pigtails, and providing plenty of scenes in which his eyes bugged out, he ate chicken, or burst into frightened-but-comical tears. Contemporary comics, like Eddie Murphy and Richard Pryor, have certainly done some great work in their careers, but they have also, on occasion, played into and played up their roles as "trickster" figures—that stereotypical role in which blacks are fast-and-loose hucksters, forever getting into jams, forever jive-talking their way out of them. While Richard Pryor's early stand-up work is brilliant, *The Toy* (1982), in which he plays a penniless writer hired by a rich white man to be his spoiled child's human play-thing, was rife with stereotype. Eddie Murphy played the trickster jive-talking role in the original *Beverly Hills Cop* (before he attained the box-office clout to get the upper hand on his on-screen relationship with Nick Nolte in *48 Hours*), and Chris Tucker has played the role in almost every one of his movies, notably *Money Talks* (in which he played a hustler opposite Charlie Sheen), and *Rush Hour* (in which he toned down his high-pitched motormouth a bit, although only in the first sequel). Sometimes the stereotypes are exported to noncomedy fare. In the sci-fi movie *Fifth Element* (1997), Tucker, who is a genuinely talented comic who just needs to apply himself a bit better, plays some sort of androgynous space creature who bugs his eyes out constantly—*Our Gang* for the twenty-second century.

Strictly Business changes the rules of film comedy. In this movie, the "trickster" character is black, but he doesn't want to be a trickster anymore, and the straight man is a black man who is trying to learn a few trickster moves. The plot is this: Waymon (Joseph C. Phillips) is a black real estate executive trying to make partner; Bobby (Tommy Davidson) is a mailroom clerk trying to make it into the management trainee program. Waymon agrees to help Bobby, if Bobby will help him win the heart of Natalie (Halle). The two cooperate in the boardroom, and the final message is one of black empowerment. Bobby even helps Waymon recruit some heavy-hitting black investors for a big business deal.

Hooks told me: "To me it always felt like a throwback kind of film. It always felt to me that we were doing a film in the vein of the 1960s comedies that I grew up on—like with Elvis, and Frankie Avalon and Annette Funicello. From a story standpoint we weren't telling anything new. But we were dealing with characters that in black films we hadn't necessarily seen."

Davidson is extremely funny throughout the film, firing off one-liners that are smart and sharp. His line readings move to a hip-hop beat, but he never pulls a Chris Tucker and starts bugging his eyes out. Halle's role is a modest one, but she makes a strong impression. In her first scene the camera caresses her body in slow motion as she walks through a restaurant; in another, the camera circles around her as she dances in the club. The movie successfully captures her radiance, her energy, her youth. You take one look at her and think: This is a big star.

Hooks told me that "the camera loves her. I wish I could take credit for that being some sort of cinematic formula, that I had to shoot her in a specific way to get those results. But the reality is the camera loves her. It's hard to make Halle look bad. Some people have been successful in that—in *Jungle Fever* she didn't go the glamorous route but she's so radiant and the camera picks up on every ounce of that. I wasn't surprised but I was overwhelmed by what she was giving out." The film is also full of future notables, including Samuel L. Jackson as the mailroom boss, Isaiah Washington as a guy in a club, James McDaniel *(NYPD Blue)* as a businessman, and Dennis Leary as a club owner.

Like the 1988 Melanie Griffith comedy *Working Girl, Strictly Business* is an opinionated take on office life. *Working Girl* was meant as a cinematic expression of solidarity for white women, but *Strictly Business* takes it even further: It's a movie for black men and black women to bond over. The comedy of dysfunction and destruction is easy; it's much harder to make funny, constructive, romantic, and yet still hip comedy, because you can't just go for cheap laughs. *Strictly Business* is a terrific comedy—and it's a shame that Warner Bros., at the time of this writing, has not yet issued it on DVD. In fact, a surprising number of great black films are only available on video, and not DVD.

Strictly Business performed admirably at the box office given its modest budget (cost: under $4 million), pulling in $7,683,000.

Halle also reportedly found romance—and heartbreak—with a fellow actor around this time. *Strictly Business* was filmed in New York City; the cast was loose and young and the film itself featured cameos from music acts, including the R and B singing group Jodeci. Members of the cast would hang out, go to concerts, have a good time; in particular, Halle became close with co-star Tommy Davidson, and the two would have dinners together and go clubbing. That was the fun side of Halle's life then.

In 1991, according to a production assistant who worked with Halle on *Strictly Business* and who was quoted in *People* magazine, a failed romance with Wesley Snipes left her "crying all the time."

Boomerang is another underappreciated romantic comedy. Made by the filmmaking Hudlin brothers (Warrington produces, Reginald directs), it was the first big-budget film about upper-middle-class blacks. I interviewed the Hudlins when the movie was first released in 1992. In June 2002, ten years later, I talked to Warrington again to get his perspective on Halle Berry and the making of the film.

The first story Warrington told me was about Halle's audition: "She came in and she was fabulous. She was unbelievable. But you have to give Eddie Murphy choices, he has approval of his co-stars. So she came in to basically do a scene with Eddie, the scene where she breaks up with him. And let me tell you, she came with fire. She blazed him so bad, at the end of the scene he just turned away and walked to the corner and put his head in the corner until she left. And then when the door shut he turned to me and my brother and said 'I don't want to see any other actors, she's got the part.' I said, 'But Eddie there are other people in the waiting room, waiting to come in.' He said, 'I told you, I don't want to see anybody else, she's got the part.' He actually caused me some ill will with some other actors who are talented. I had to go out to the waiting room and say 'Everyone else go home.' But he just refused to see anyone else. She brought him to the ground. The scene she did was unbelievable."

Boomerang tells the story of New York marketing executive Marcus Graham (played by Eddie Murphy). Graham has a taste for good food, fine clothes, and an insatiable appetite for good-looking women. Because he's suave, smart, and sophisticated he gets his fair share of dates, but he can never settle on the right one, even rejecting one beautiful woman because her feet are "funky." Marcus gets his comeuppance when he meets up with another high-powered ad executive, Jacquelyn (played by Robin Givens), who is smarter, more sophisticated, and even more ruthless when it comes to sexual relationships. Soon, however, Marcus finds himself falling for Angela Lewis (Halle), Jacquelyn's sweet assistant.

Reginald Hudlin told the *Chicago Tribune* in 1992: "There are things I love to see [Eddie] do. But there were also all these things I wanted to see him do. Like: I wanted to see him hanging out with his buddies, because I always thought Eddie would have funny buddies. So he's got two friends that he spends a lot of time with. And I wanted to see him in a romance. So we got Robin Givens and Halle Berry."

"*Boomerang* is a very political film," Eddie Murphy said in the *Los Angeles Times* in 1992. "Because it is black and yet it's about nothing to do with being black and it cost $40 million. So if it's successful, then it will prove that you can do [mainstream] movies about blacks that are not just set in the 'hood. Those movies are good, but if that's all we did—if every time a movie came out and it was 'Hey man, it's goin' down'—then we'd be right back in exploitation films again."

Warrington told me that making the movie was an adventure. "The movie was continually rewritten. The first script was so wack, so horrible, that when the writers came to the screening they didn't know what was going to happen next—we deviated so much from the original plot. So we would complain to Eddie. We would rewrite, rewrite, rewrite, rewrite, and we'd say 'Eddie, we need to do more' and he'd say 'It's fine,' and he'd come in the next morning and say, 'This script sucks.' We'd say 'We told you that sh— last night.' So for the first hour of the day, Eddie, my brother, and I would go into the trailer and come out with a rewrite. Then you combine that with the improvisation that was going on."

Halle was a bright spot in the difficult shoot. "She is the sweetest person," Warrington said to me. "Normally everyone rushes to the trailer. She would eat with the crew, she would sit down with the grips and the gaffers. She is such a regular down-to-earth accessible person. It just shocked me how sweet she was. She's good people. But then you meet her mother and she's so sweet and down-to-earth you go, okay, that's where it came from."

Halle, for her part, got her first front-row look at a major star at work. And she didn't like everything she saw. She thought Murphy was nice, but also thought he was bitter. Murphy told her that he was waging battles with Paramount on the film that she couldn't see, that she wasn't even aware of, but Halle felt he and the studio just needed to straighten out whatever it was that was going on between them. "Eddie is a star and lives the big-star life, which was really interesting because that's totally not my thing," Halle informed London's *Daily Mail* in 1993. "All the bodyguards and the whole star trip is not my scene." She went on: "It was the first time I was exposed to that. I found it interesting rather than funny because I did see situations where maybe Eddie needed those five bodyguards because sometimes women would just come up, mobs of them, and try to attack him. But he had all these people living in his house and I felt it would be a drag."

Halle builds her character smartly in *Boomerang*. In her first scene, she doesn't even say a word, all she does is smile sweetly at Marcus when they are introduced at a party. At the close of the movie, she shows her fire, telling off Marcus in a memorable scene. Marcus has just spent the night with his former lover, Jacquelyn. Angela gets in his face—not just jabbing at him with her finger but pushing his forehead back with it. Her anger is palpable, and seeing this gentle soul explode makes the scene even more visceral. Marcus continues to plead his case, prompting Angela to slap him. It is a fine slap, as such things go, and the audience feels it. Halle seems to follow that slap with several more blows using just her eyes.

Most mainstream critics weren't kind to the film, which was nonetheless a box-office success. It grossed $70 million domestically, which was okay for an Eddie Murphy movie, and unprecedented for a film directed and produced by African-American filmmakers. Nonetheless, many critics seemed to think the enclave of upscale blacks portrayed in the film was unrealistic; many wanted to see Murphy in more familiar roles as a hustler or scoundrel. In a July 1, 1992, review, *Los Angeles Times* critic Kenneth Turan lamented the fact that Murphy's upscale character was "no hustler, no scrambler after respectability, he is a polished and successful director of marketing for a successful cosmetics corporation." The review also attacked the all-black cast, saying: "On one level, this kind of cinematic affirmative action can be seen as long overdue, but . . . it feels in its own way as silly and arbitrary as mainstream movies without any people of color on the screen." He conceded that Berry is "appealing."

Eddie Murphy, in an essay published in the *Los Angeles Times* on July 20, 1992, entitled "All We Want Is Equal Treatment," fired back: "I must say that Hollywood is finally—although slowly—opening its eyes to the great, diverse pool of black talent. Yet for every step we inch forward, for each iota of progress, there always will be those trying to knock us back down, and there always will be some who cannot accept our success. My new film *Boomerang*, directed and produced by the aforementioned Hudlins, is the latest outlet for those critics who feel it necessary to demean and simplify the achievement of black people. . . . *Boomerang* is a romantic comedy revolving around the lives of successful black people who work for a successful black company. Some people obviously have a problem with that, for the movie has been called a 'fantasy' a 'reverse world' and 'racist.' For those who feel that it's racist for a film to have a predominantly black cast, one has only to look at the countless movies that portray an all-white world."

Murphy concluded: "For those who cannot rise above their own ignorance and admit to themselves that there are indeed successful black companies in this country, I suggest a review of the *Black Enterprise* magazine's annual BE 100. The top five black-owned companies on this list generated sales of more than $2 billion—that's billion—in 1991. . . . *Boomerang* is a movie. For the most part, movies are fantasy. But I cannot be more passionate when I say that the situations found in this film are *not* from some fictional dream world. Until everyone can realize this, the cancerous roots of racism will continue to spread, and the people of this country will continue to be torn apart and destroyed by the disease of misunderstanding."

Warrington, ten years later, still smarts at the memory of some of the reviews of his movie. "Reviews are very valuable. It was really a Rorschach blot for white America. We moved Eddie Murphy and the persona of Eddie Murphy into a new realm. He became no longer the trickster coon figure—which they love—he became the romantic comedic lead that Cary Grant made a career of being. There was a real discomfort that Eddie Murphy no longer knew his place, we as filmmakers didn't know our place and we had encroached into a genre that was really only a white-only area. Everyone in the movie was good-looking and upscale and that wasn't how blacks were supposed to perform in the industry."

"What was exciting for us is that a black star empowered me and my brother. Once we were empowered we had $40 million to do it the way we wanted to do it. And any time the studio tried to push us, we had this big giant name Eddie Murphy who would protect us. So it's a cinematic vision that comes out of the life that we lead. And therefore we were free of the shackles of these conventional depictions of black life. We didn't have to run through the formulas that Hollywood had laid out for black folks. And that's why the movie has such emotional resonance for black folks and caused consternation for white people."

Warrington, who is a mild-mannered Ivy League–educated guy, concluded, "This is going to sound conspiratorial, so forgive me. There was a concerted effort to make *Boomerang* not perceived as a success because if it did, that means a black star, forming an alliance with black filmmakers, is a good thing. They prefer that white producers, white writers, white directors have the management and execution of these black filmmakers' storytelling careers. There was a concerted effort to disparage what we have accomplished because it was too threatening to the racial economy of Hollywood."

Despite the attacks of some critics and Hollywood insiders, *Boomerang* put Halle Berry on an upscale trajectory. She didn't want to do *Boyz N the Hood* rip-offs. In fact, she turned down a role in *Menace II Society* (which, actually, turned out to be a great film—as fierce and as artfully directed as Martin Scorsese's *Mean Streets,* the film that helped launch a young Robert De Niro). Halle said to the *Dallas Morning News* in 1993: "We've got *Boyz N the Hood* and *New Jack City,* and those are definitely stories we've got to tell. But we as black people have many more stories. It would bug me to know that the only story that people want to see is crime and drugs. I'm hoping they find other life experiences just as interesting."

In 1994, Halle told *Movieline:* "Look, we black African Americans or whatever term is correct, feel like we've reached equality, sometimes, in certain areas. But filmmaking isn't one of them. 'Black Films' quote unquote? Black exploitation films, if you ask me. It's not only no different from the *Shaft* era, it's even worse. The nature of these movies is that they're so violent, they deal with such negative subject matter we're not willing to pay money to see them. Just turn on the news."

Ironically, even as she rejected violent films, Halle's personal life was struck by chaos. Around the early 1990s she began dating a man who physically abused her, hitting her so hard she lost 80 percent of the hearing in her right ear. Halle has never named the man. She admitted to London's *Daily Mail* in 1993: "I'd been in a few bad relationships. I took whoever chose me and often they weren't right and, on one occasion, abusive. I got hit in the ear by a man in a past relationship and I don't have hearing in one ear. I was real docile and passive and would never assert myself. He knows what he's done."

Halle's story on this incident has changed somewhat from year to year, from interview to interview. She has, on occasion, admitted that she was in several relationships that were abusive, mentally and physically, and not just one. One man she dumped began to stalk her, sending her dead snakes in the mail and other strange things. It's also difficult to tell how much she blames herself for her romantic problems, perhaps unfairly. She has also said that in the relationship with the man who abused her, that blows were thrown on both sides—as if to spread the culpability.

It's pretty obvious, though, that Halle (a slightly built five feet six inches) is fairly incapable of really hurting most men, unless you count breaking their hearts.

Over the years there has been rampant speculation over the identity of the boyfriend who struck Halle and impaired her hearing. The names of some major Hollywood stars have been thrown around and at least one celebrity magazine has even questioned a male star in print and asked if he was the man who abused Halle (the male star denied it). Halle herself has said that she has vowed never to disclose the man's name or even discuss the incident in detail in the press, though she did tell *Redbook* that her assailant was "well known" in Hollywood.

In her mind, it seems, love and anger are still intertwined. Even after the man's alleged assault, even after the end of the relationship, even in the wake of her permanent injury, Halle has decided that because she once loved this man, whoever he is, she owes him some loyalty. She seemingly believes that once you love, you never stop loving. So she will not stigmatize the man by revealing his name.

Clearly, Halle Berry, after the end of this abusive relationship, was an emotional work in progress. But a man was about to enter her life who would change everything.

"My ex-husband and I fell in love
at first sight. Maybe I should have
taken a second look."

—MIA FARROW IN
Crimes and Misdemeanors

"The minute I met Dave Justice,
my life was over."

—HALLE BERRY

FOUR

No Justice

She saw him on television. She was a star already; many young men had seen her on the small screen, or on the silver screen, and had dreams of her. Now, seeing this muscular, mocha-colored man spread out on her set, she was the one doing the dreaming. It was just a silly little show she was watching, something on MTV—what was it called?—oh yes, Rock 'n' Jock. Athletes and entertainers playing a game together. She couldn't quite figure out the rules to the game and she couldn't quite make out the point, but the man was fine. The announcer said his name and she took note of it and, a few days later, she called a friend. "Who is David Justice?" "He plays for the Braves." She didn't know much about baseball and didn't know anything about the Braves but she couldn't stop thinking about this man. Here she was, just out of a bad relationship and already dreaming about another one. Over the phone line, her friend told her to take it slow, take a break, stay away from another potential love mistake. "Halle," her friend said, "don't go chasing after a man.

Let love find you." It sounded like good advice, and Lord knows she had enough on her plate. But she couldn't stop thinking about that man: Who was David Justice?

This is not a love story. Black love stories are hard to find. Hollywood certainly isn't even looking.

There are thousands of love stories that don't feature blacks—Charlie Chaplin's sweet and silent *City Lights,* Katharine Hepburn and Humphrey Bogart's *The African Queen* (a movie that, by the way, has nothing to do with Africans or African Americans), Robert Redford and Meryl Streep's *Out of Africa* (another movie that has nothing to do with Africans or African Americans), Billy Crystal and Meg Ryan's goofy *When Harry Met Sally* (a film which, although set in New York City, features virtually no minorities of any sort).

Hollywood screenwriters can dream up aliens and wizards, robots and superheroes but black love seems strangely beyond them. Black love stories in Hollywood are even rarer than black directors and black screenwriters and black cinematographers. There's Diana Ross's *Mahogany*—another film that made money but, at the time of this writing, is still not available on DVD; *Love and Basketball,* a small film about a female b-baller and a male b-baller who fall for each other (it's better than it sounds); and there's *Love Jones,* another small, smart film about a black novelist and a black poet who have a romance. There's also *Brown Sugar,* a terrific hip-hop fla-vored romance that came out in 2002.

There aren't that many more full-out black romantic movies, not quality ones anyway, and certainly not thousands (yes, I could name a handful of others, such as *How Stella Got Her Groove Back,* but there aren't many more). Sidney Poitier was one of Hollywood's greatest black stars, but the only major love story he ever did was the interracial comedy *Guess Who's Coming to Dinner?* (In the 1965 melodrama *A Patch of Blue,* a white woman falls for Poitier's character, but, of course, she's visually impaired, apparently the only kind of woman Hollywood execs could imagine going for a handsome black man. *Newsweek* wrote of the movie at the time "no other film has managed to simultaneously insult the Negroes and the blind.")

Denzel Washington is one of Hollywood's hand-somest leading men, but he's only starred in two roman-tic movies in his career—the interracial Indian/African-American love story *Mississippi Masala* (another truly fantastic film unavailable on DVD) and Spike Lee's jazzy drama *Mo' Better Blues.* When Washington starred with Julia Roberts in *The Pelican Brief,* he didn't even get a peck on the cheek (although there was a love affair in the original script).

Halle Berry is perhaps Hollywood's most beautiful and desirable actress, and yet she's only appeared in two love stories, both near the beginning of her career, both directed by black filmmakers—*Strictly Business* and *Boomerang.* She did co-star in a television movie called *The Wedding* in 1998, but interestingly enough, that project was about an interracial affair. Now, of course,

all love—white, interracial, whatever—should be celebrated. But why is black love almost completely ignored
by movie studios? It's almost as if once Halle got big,
Hollywood wanted to keep her away from love, away
from black on-screen suitors.

So this is not a love story. Just as there is a lack of love
in her profession, Halle, throughout her life, has been
just as lacking for romance in her private life.
Throughout her career, despite her beauty, despite her
status as a sex symbol, despite her very public search for
the right mate, her film choices have almost consistently
excluded love. It's lamentable whenever someone fails to
find that perfect person in his or her real life; it's perhaps
just as sad when they can't even imagine the possibility
of love in their fantasy life.

In 1992 I went to Hollywood to meet Halle Berry,
but I was about as far from California as you could get—
Halle was shooting the miniseries *Queen* in Hollywood,
South Carolina. It was during the full heat of summer. It
was a steam heat that turned your forehead into a faucet,
soaked through your shirt, and left you, every few paces,
dreaming of cool fans and cold sodas in Upstate New
York. This Hollywood was very far away from the other
Hollywood. About ten miles down the road from where
Halle was filming, there was a prominently posted
"David Duke for President" sign—apparently, more than
a few local residents were big supporters of the former
Klansman's infamous presidential bid.

This Hollywood was about thirteen miles outside
of Charleston. The crew, when I got there, was camped

outside a muddy pond. There was one crew member whose job it was to beat away alligators with a stick. I don't think there's an Oscar category for that job, but there should be. I was there to talk to Halle for *USA Today*, and during a break from a long day of shooting, she came over to me. *Queen* was a period piece, and she walked over to me still dressed in her heavy nine-teenth-century-style brown dress. Helped by two people, she lowered herself (or rather, she was lowered) into a chair.

As it turned out, Halle filmed *Queen* under duress. There was a lot going on in her life. The month before, she fell off a horse and injured her back ("Actually, it's called the coccyx bone," she told me then). After that accident, the production was shut down for almost two weeks. Danny Glover, one of her co-stars on the project, nearly dropped out. But Halle had fought hard to land the part, and didn't want to see the production die. She started showing up for work in an ambulance. Halle told me then, laughing: "I've had to get cortisone shots and shots of novocaine, pain pills. I'll be a drug addict by the time this is over."

Queen was one of the biggest black film projects ever—it was a six-hour, three-part CBS miniseries and Halle was the title character. The miniseries, based on the writings and research of Alex Haley, told the epic story of Queen Haley, the daughter of a black slave woman and a white slave master. Queen was paternal grandmother to Alex, who told the story of the other side of his family tree in the book and miniseries *Roots*.

Queen was based on the manuscript Haley was working on when he died in February 1992.

Halle, being biracial herself, felt an intimate connection to the project. Also, given the fact that the writer and chief inspiration for the project had recently passed away, she felt an added responsibility to tell the story in a way that did respect to its origins. This was the most important project she had ever done. She knew that everyone was watching—agents, managers, directors, producers, studio heads, the public, her mother, and maybe even Alex Haley himself from on high—and she didn't want to win such a big opportunity and then squander it, only to have all those old doubts about her talent and whether she was just another pretty face and not much more all surface again with new velocity and veracity. "*Queen* is much more meaningful to me than a *Strictly Business* or a *Boomerang* or a *Last Boy Scout,*" Halle told me, rattling off the names of some of her other movies. "It's a big responsibility to black people and just people in general."

She fell in love with *Queen* from the moment she read the script. She felt as if she was born to do the part. She told the *Cleveland Plain Dealer* in 1993: "I read the script and was so passionate about it that I wanted it more than anything so far in my career. It was the most challenging thing I've ever done and probably will ever do as an actress."

She went on: "And it was a lot of pressure. The minute after I found out I was given the part, my manager told me I had a meeting with John Erman, the director, to discuss everything. And I broke down in tears and said, 'I don't want to go, I'm scared, I don't want to go!' For the first time, the pressure of carrying a six-hour movie sort of hit me. I didn't quite know how I'd get through it."

Halle, who had gone through so much racial turmoil in her life, saw this as her chance—perhaps her only chance, you never know—to tell her story through someone else, to investigate her own past through American history, and perhaps teach viewers—black, white, mixed, and others—what being multiracial in America was all about. "If they watch it, I think they'll leave with an education," she told me then, "and it may help our racial problems that we have today, dealing with the black-white issue and it may help us realize how crazy it all is."

Halle truly felt she was on a mission. She was even seeing things—supernatural things, inexplicable things—that she linked to fate. She told me that in photos of her taken in costume, there was a white haze around her, as if some spirit was hovering nearby. Also, in photos, one of Halle's eyes appeared slightly bigger than the other, just like Queen Haley, whose eyes were of slightly different sizes. I didn't quite believe all these stories, but Halle's passion was unmistakeably real. She said to me: "I think something's been guiding me from the day I read the script."

Queen's story, like Halle's story, is partly about race. But Queen, unlike Halle, was confused about who she was. Was she white or was she black? Could she ever find happiness on one side or the other or was she destined to dwell in misery in the in-betweens? There are some fairly big stars in *Queen* (well, big for the small screen anyway), including Ossie Davis, Martin Sheen, Ann-Margret, Danny Glover, Jasmine Guy *(A Different World)*, and Tim Daly *(Wings)*. The problem with the series is partly due to its protagonist—Queen seems to be more a victim of circumstance and history than a great heroic figure. She's not leading slaves to freedom on the Underground Railroad, she's journeying into herself. Her biggest dilemma is her choice, whether she should be black or white. Her efforts to pass and to integrate into white society come across as small and pitiful, not grandly tragic. The screenplay by David Stevens lacks wit and insight; nobody delivers any lines worth remembering and actors seem to be fighting with the turgid dialogue rather than working with it.

Another key problem with *Queen* is Halle herself— her performance seems desperate and not deeply felt; perhaps because she cared so much about the part, she lost her sense of nuance and balance. "I was being slapped around and raped on screen, but I was going through my own torment off-screen as well," Halle said to London's *Daily Mail* in 1993. "Towards the end I was such a wreck that no one wanted to be around me. I was a bitch. I was biting everybody's heads off. I had lived this woman's life from the age of 15 to 65 as she was sexually abused, beaten, treated like dirt. I really felt the injustice and I was called nigger just one time too many on screen. It was all too much and after three and a half months on the shoot I began to take it too personally, which you don't want to do, but if you're a sensitive human being who has emotions and feelings then it's difficult not to let some of those tears be real." In the end, her off-screen problems seeped into her on-screen work, and not in a good way. Sometimes an actor can draw from pain, sometimes it can draw from the actor. The horse-riding accident, the racial baggage, the career pressure—it all seemed to get to Halle during *Queen.* For the first time, she seems like a model trying to act.

Many critics panned *Queen,* and the public wasn't happy with it either. While there was a hunger to explore some of the issues *Queen* explored, such as the challenges faced by biracial America, there was a sense that this miniseries, and its star, had squandered an opportunity. "*Queen* is just not believable," Olivia Toatley, a sixth-grade public school teacher told the *Washington Post* in 1993. "The actors playing the younger roles just didn't have the depth. Maybe because I have this image of Halle Berry. She's just not old enough, hasn't lived enough to play the part."

After the series wrapped, Halle was still in turmoil. When the Emmys were announced and she was passed over, it slashed at her insides. She had given everything to this part, and yet here she was again, unrecognized, unhonored—once again a prom queen without a prom. "We were told so little about slavery at school. The whole South went into economic ruin when slavery was abolished, but not too many people know what went on. I was bitter and just mad at people when I got through the TV series," Halle once said, describing her feelings at the time. For a few minutes, thoughts of suicide crossed her mind. Said Halle: "So I got some therapy after the show just to get me back in touch. The therapist helped me work through all those emotions and helped me understand what it all meant. He told me to scream and get all the anger I felt out of my system. I had gone to him thinking I was going to give up acting and become a full-time civil rights activist. It took me two months to get myself back to reality, if you can call Los Angeles reality."

There's another possible reason for why Halle's performance in *Queen* was so powerfully mediocre: His name was David Justice. Remember, this is *not* a love story. Love can enhance a career. Ossie Davis and Ruby Dee support each other, play off each other, and have even acted in a number of films together, including *Do the Right Thing* and *Jungle Fever*. Paul Newman and Joanne Woodward and Tim Robbins and Susan Sarandon are other married couples whose careers seemed to have been enhanced by their union. Of course, there are too many celebrities to name here who have gone through the opposite of romance or have had romance take away from the work, their lives, their images. Halle would soon discover that her new flame could warm her life and singe it as well.

But remember, this is not a love story.

Halle met David Justice on television. She was relaxing from filming *Queen*, watching television in her room when she saw him on an MTV program called *Rock 'n' Jock*. David Justice, baseball slugger. She took mental note. Not long afterward, Halle had a serendipitous meeting. Halle informed London's *Daily Mail* in 1993: "A friend of his was interviewing me, and David had asked for my autograph. I had seen him on television playing baseball so I knew who he was. So I said to the interviewer: 'Here's the autograph and give him my telephone number as well.' He rang within the hour and two weeks after that we met and I knew the minute I saw him face-to-face that I was going to marry him."

She had to see through a lot to see the man she wanted. Justice, that first day, was dressed like a parody of a big-time sports star: He had on necklaces and bracelets; he had rings on every finger and earrings on both ears. But Halle thought she saw a different person beneath all the glitter and gold. She thought she felt a warmth, thought she sensed something comforting and gentle. She even told him right off: All the jewelry wasn't him. He agreed, and said he realized he was playing a part. "This was a time when I got to choose my man," Halle said in 1993. "I recognized a gentle quality in David and I said the next man has got to have some real tender qualities because I didn't want to fear that he was going to hit me. He's got these big dimples and big warm smile. He wouldn't hurt a fly." Halle gushed even more to the *Cleveland Plain Dealer* in 1993. "The minute I met Dave Justice my life was over. I can't go anywhere with this man without being bombarded by fans. I'm used to that being around him." She also liked the fact that he had his mother's name tattooed on his arm, something he told her during their first phone conversation. Halle would later get David's name tattooed on her back.

In 1994, Justice told a reporter for *Sports Illustrated* that his union with Halle was destiny. Said Justice: "I knew when I first saw her that I was going to marry her. It's like I heard a voice. 'This is going to be your wife,' something inside me said." Justice went on to make a strange analogy as to why he and Halle were fated to be together: "Like when I was 15 coming home from school. I put my hand through a door window and cut my wrist right here. I severed the tendon. The doctor said if it had been a half inch deeper I wouldn't have been able to use my hand for two years. Half an inch to the right and it would have cut my main artery and I would have been dead. But it didn't happen like that. And you know why it didn't? It wasn't meant to be."

Justice seemed to have led a charmed life; it was not free from hardship, from struggle, but, like Halle's life, he always seemed to come out of tough times successfully. He grew up in Covington, Kentucky, a small town near the Ohio border. His father, Robert Justice, left home when David was just four years old. He was raised by his mother, Nettie, who was a housekeeper for a wealthy white family. But David doesn't remember wanting for anything—athletic equipment, clothes, even a moped. "I grew up great and had everything I wanted," David told *Sports Illustrated* in 1994.

David was a smart kid, with an IQ of more than 140;

he skipped the seventh and eighth grades and graduated from Covington High at sixteen years of age. He was also a cool kid, with a rep for staying calm under pressure—his nickname was "Ice Man." He attended Thomas More College in Crestview Hills, Kentucky, but he left early. In 1985 he was drafted by the Atlanta Braves in the fourth round as a free agent. A few years later, after doing time in farm teams, the six-foot, two-inch, 200-pound slugger/outfielder began paying dividends—in 1990 he hit twenty-eight homers and was named the National League's Rookie of the Year. The next year, though, his attitude began to change. He rolled up to spring training in a Mercedes with a vanity plate that read "Sweet Swing." He began wearing more gold, more furs, more jewelry. He stopped giving as many autographs, and stopped being as open with his teammates. And he stopped being as good a baseball player.

Breaking tradition, Halle had been the one to propose to Justice. Even David's mother was swept up in the romance, saying, "We couldn't have found a better bride if we had ordered one from Sears and Roebuck." After a honeymoon at a secluded Caribbean resort, Halle threw herself into her most challenging role to date: baseball wife. She didn't really like Atlanta, but she liked spending time with David in Atlanta. She didn't really like baseball, but she liked keeping David happy and doing that meant she had to learn to love what can be an aggressively boring sport. Halle told *Playboy* in 1994: "I had to make a real effort at first. Those games are long. At my first baseball game, I was ready to go after an hour. Once I started to learn about the game—the intricate parts of it, the pitches, the plays, how to keep score—that made the time go by. Now I can sit through a three-hour game and think wow, where did the time go?"

Meanwhile, Halle had a career to oversee. After yet another battle with filmmakers, she landed the role of Sharon Stone in a big-budget live-action version of the old TV series *The Flintstones*. The role was originally written for the *real* Sharon Stone, but Halle fought for the part and landed it, convincing the filmmakers behind the movie that Bedrock should be integrated. "People don't really, really seek me out," Halle told the *Atlanta Journal-Constitution*. "Even with *The Flintstones*, I had to hear about it. They didn't ask to see me. But when I read it I thought, I could play this. I mean, this girl wasn't in the original cartoon. Bedrock should be integrated. This character could be me if they'll see me. It's a comedy, you know, let's see if they can take a joke. And I got the role."

In June 2002, I talked to Brian Levant, the director of *The Flintstones*, about working with Halle. The first topic we covered: Was the part of Sharon Stone really meant for Sharon Stone originally? Levant answered: "Yes, Steven Spielberg [the executive producer of *The Flintstones*] envisioned it that way. She made a very poor decision and took a film the title of which I can't even remember and I'm sure I'm not alone it that. And that opened the door for a lot of people. To tell you the truth, the way Halle got the part was we had so many choices that we went back and watched a compilation tape of everyone who had come in and it was only then that she totally blew us away.

"The first thing that Halle said when she came in to read for us is 'I didn't know there were black people in Bedrock.' And in the original Flintstone series there weren't. But in all the subsequent ones, Hanna-Barbara studios got with the times and integrated—just for backgrounds. I told her 'Hey, we know where life started—in Africa.' So there better be black people in Bedrock."

He went on: "It has been cited many times as color-blind casting and that's partially true. The fact that she shown so brightly in the audition allowed us to add some ethnic diversity, which we wanted to do. But it wasn't the driving force [as to why she was cast]. The performance was the driving force. We took the tape over to Amblin and showed it to Steven Spielberg and he knew Halle because she'd participated in some sort of program where they bring writers in and actors to perform their scenes. He'd seen her work up close and thought it was a great choice. After that all I needed to do was make a call to business affairs."

Halle took some grief from people about doing a mainstream family film. Halle told *Playboy* in 1994: "It's amazing how people can be so negative. Some people have said to me '*The Flintstones?* That's a cartoon. I thought you wanted to be a serious actor. You just did *Queen.* I mean, Halle!' But not everything's going to be

Queen or *Malcolm X.* This film is really important to me because to be a black woman and be the object of everybody's else desire in this movie is such a coup. The fact that these executives at the studio, who are all white males, took the risk to have a black woman as this character says a lot as to where we're going. No, we don't want to be just sex objects or be just beautiful. But the level of consciousness is being raised, and that's important to me. We're starting to be seen a little bit differently."

The Flintstones is a trifle of a movie. It's one of those comic adaptations, like the Batman series, where everything—the actors, the plot, the dialogue—seems weighed down by the costumes. Some of the casting works—John Goodman as Fred Flintstone seems appropriate—but the rest of the actors seem strained. Halle, as a villain with a heart of gold, looks great in a series of belly button–bearing animal-skin outfits. Halle didn't deserve an Oscar for her glorified cameo in *The Flintstones,* but she at least deserved a pet rock.

Although Halle's character is a villain, she makes a turn near the end and becomes sympathetic. Says Levant: "That was [Spielberg's] influence; he thought she should be redeemed at the end. I had originally fought it, to tell you the truth, but finally I think it worked out great. People liked her so much they didn't want her to be bad. He just had a feeling that there shouldn't be more than one bad guy in a Flintstones movie. I thought that was a little easy. But it worked out well for the film."

The Flintstones, despite its flaws as a movie, was an

enormous hit, making $130 million domestically, $228 million outside the United States, and some $71 million in rentals. Its box-office success allowed Halle, for the first time, to add a $100 million hit to her résumé, one of the signs of a true superstar.

The movie was accompanied by one major disappointment for Halle, however. She was left out of the merchandising. Levant told me: "Although we had cautioned the toymakers at Mattel that, for instance, in *Jurassic Park* I don't think they had any black character in their toys, we warned them on *The Flintstones:* 'You really should make a Halle Berry doll'—but they didn't want to make that many. So they made an arbitrary cut there and I think she was a little upset by that. They didn't make a Halle Berry doll and they should have. I saw that she had been disappointed that there weren't toys of her. They had Fred, Wilma, Barney, Betty, Kyle [McLachlan] who was the villain, and Dino. Even Dino. And they were not successful sellers I might add."

Next, Halle scored a juicy role opposite Jessica Lange in the drama *Losing Isaiah*. Like *Queen,* it was a movie with a theme that was close to her heart. "I could definitely relate," Berry said to the *Atlanta Journal-Constitution* in 1994. "The issues that are brought up, especially in the court scenes, were really important. Can this white family give this little black child the history, the culture, that he needs to have? And can they do things like comb his hair? You know, knowing the differences in texture between a black person's hair and a white person's hair.

The different products that black people use in their hair. I mean, little things like that seem really minute, but in the scheme of things they can become really important."

Losing Isaiah has a terrific cast—Jessica Lange, David Strathairn, Cuba Gooding Jr., and Samuel L. Jackson—who struggle mightily to bring some life to a story that is as stiff as a day-old corpse. A scene where Strathairn has to admit in court to an infidelity is particularly sharp—watching Strathairn's face register, in succession, surprise, anger, and numb acceptance is worth the price of this movie. The core of the story has promise: a crack addict (Halle) leaves her son in the garbage and the baby is adopted by a white doctor (Lange) and her husband (Strathairn). After Halle's character cleans up her life, she takes Lange's character and her husband to court to get back her child. There are some provocative issues raised: What's more important, culture or financial stability? Does race matter in raising a child? Do bad parents deserve second chances? Unfortunately none of the issues is examined with much intelligence.

Halle gives a solid performance, though she was better and more effective in the small role as an addict in *Jungle Fever*. There's a fine, fierce scene in which Halle and Lange square off in a bathroom during a court break—Lange's haggard, bitter line readings are impressive and moving and Halle holds her ground.

One of Halle's many talents is that she can act hard and hurt at the same time. Even when she expresses anger with her words, her eyes register her suffering;

Halle, time and time again, strikes chords of feeling. Another of Halle's abilities is that she can act "down" without acting down; in other words, she can adopt street argot and hip-hop phrasing in her voice without seeming like it's a put-on or a pose. Many middle-class actors can't do it without seeming uncomfortable.

After *Losing Isaiah* wrapped, Halle had some residual bitterness over the way she had been treated on the set. "When I'm on a movie set, I try to be cooperative," Halle said to *Essence* in 1996. "I say thank you and please, and I expect the same in return. But when I was called a bitch by a production assistant, I went off. Don't try to make me feel lucky to be here, because I've worked damn hard and I've got the goods. I still have to convince managers and agents that they should send me out for the next level of scripts. I don't want to abandon black filmmakers, but I don't want to keep doing 'girls in the 'hood' either."

Losing Isaiah failed to capitalize on the promise of its stellar cast and provocative theme. It took in only $7,603,000. The film cost $17 million to make.

One of Halle's most enjoyable, and least remembered, films is the action thriller *Executive Decision*. The plot is this: Arab terrorists take control of a passenger plane and try to crash it into the White House. Although made long before the real-life tragedy of September 11, 2001, the movie's story line eerily foreshadows it. Halle portrays a heroic stewardess who helps a government analyst, played by Kurt Russell, foil the terrorists' plot. Halle plays her part just right, with a mixture of sweetness and steel; she seems vulnerable, but you know she's someone who is going to find inner reserves of courage when the situation calls for it. The movie has several quality surprises (including one involving Steven Seagal), and the support cast is top-notch (John Leguizamo and Joe Morton play members of a strike team). The movie loses its nerve only when it comes to romance: Kurt Russell and Halle Berry have a few flirtatious moments, but never kiss. At the end there's a winking reference to her real-life husband (Justice) to let you know she's taken: She tells Russell she prefers baseball to hockey.

Indeed, in the press at the time, Halle made a number of declarations affirming her love for her new man, but there were also hints that all was not well in her life. "I want to do this for about another six, seven years until David's through with baseball," Halle told the *Atlanta Journal-Constitution* in 1994. "And then I want to live a really different kind of life. I want to have children. I want to buy a house [on a Caribbean island] and just see a better quality of life."

Executive Decision was a mild success at the box office; it cost $55 million to make and it generated $65 million over its domestic run.

All in all, Halle was feeling good about her career—though she was, in retrospect, mistakenly optimistic about her domestic life. "If I keep getting roles in movies like *The Flintstones* and *Losing Isaiah* in the same year, five years from now I'll be fulfilled as an actress. I'll feel like I've helped open a few doors. And I'll feel like I helped bring some other black women in behind me. I would have done what my mom wanted me to do and what I wanted to do."

Celebrity romances tend to end with a scandal. Even if there isn't a real incident of wrongdoing, one will be invented. In the case of Halle and Justice, there was a bit of both. On May 13, 1996, Justice was picked up by the Riviera Beach (Florida) police for questioning when his Lexus was allegedly seen parked in an area that was reportedly known for drugs and female prostitution. Justice was due to report to spring training camp in nearby West Palm Beach, Florida, in a few hours. According to reports, police saw Justice talking to a man through the window of his Lexus and the man fled when police approached. The police report indicated that money was spread out over the passenger seat. No charges were filed, no drugs were found. Police said they released information on the incident because Justice was "well known."

In interviews, Justice voiced his outrage over the incident and his terror at being stopped by the cops. "All I could think about was Rodney King," Justice told *USA Today* in 1996. "I rolled all my windows down. I turned out all the lights. I put my hands out the window." Asked by *People* in 1996 if he ever cheated on his wife, Justice answered "absolutely not." Halle said: "If anything was going on, I didn't know about it."

Justice, in interviews, has suggested the whole incident in Florida was overblown by the press. He has been reluctant to cry "racism" but he has openly charged that other players—other white players—would not have been picked up by cops and tarnished in the press for a noncrime. One does have to wonder, though, why Justice was picked up in the first place. For merely stopping his car? Drive through almost any big city and almost any intersection can be labeled as a "place known for drugs and prostitution." That's what it means to live in a big city in America. If there aren't a few crack vials and hookers within a twenty-block radius of your home, you're probably living in a gated community, the suburbs, or Canada. Certainly it seems a little strange that police, not having charged Justice with a crime nor finding anything illicit in his possession, would release his name to the world.

In any case, not long afterward, word leaked out that the marriage was over. In the following months and years, Halle and Justice revealed that the union had been dead for some time. "I gave up my career to be with David and was made to think I had to," Halle said to London's *Mirror* in 2001. "I took a cooking class and hated it. One morning I said 'This isn't me.'" She also told *E! News Daily* the split wasn't because of lack of effort: "I'd try until I was 104 to make the marriage work, but I can't control another person."

In a series of interviews, Justice gave his take on why his marriage to Halle failed. He told *People* magazine in 1996 that he and Halle realized things were over during a trip abroad: "When we were in Bermuda for our anniversary, we both agreed we'd made a mistake with our marriage. I was unhappy. She was unhappy.

Everything I did was wrong." He opened up to *USA Today* later that same year and said that he may have gotten married too fast: "We got married seven months after we met. It was a mistake. I said 'I'll let the marriage go.' I knew what I was doing was right. I never second-guess myself. I'd never marry another celebrity again." In 1997 he confided to the *Atlanta Journal-Constitution* that timing and distance may have played a part in the breakup: "It's been something that has been kind of brewing for a while. It's tough. We've pretty much had a bicoastal relationship and didn't have a chance to spend a lot of time together. I guess those feelings kind of changed. But I love her and wish her all the best. More than anything, the timing was wrong."

The divorce was an ugly one, played out in tabloids, glossy magazines, TV entertainment programs, and even the sports pages. The public is endlessly fascinated with celebrity breakups, although they always end in the same way. The rumors. The denials. The leaks from relatives who know nothing. The leaks from publicists who know everything. The spouse seen alone. The spouse seen with someone else. The tabloids. The gossip columns. The *People* cover. The teary interview with Barbara Walters. The lawyers. The press conferences. The ugly court battle.

The Berry/Justice split climaxed with an especially ugly court battle. In the fall of 1996, Halle asked a Santa Monica judge to protect her from Justice after her soon-to-be-ex reportedly went to her Los Angeles home to retrieve some personal items. Halle recounted her version of the whole unsavory episode in court papers in September 1996:

"Approximately three (3) months ago, Respondent [David Justice] appeared at my home and demanded to come into the home. I contacted private security who came to the home and, without police intervention, both security individuals persuaded the Respondent to vacate the premises and to make arrangements, through his attorneys, to pick up whatever personal belongings he had left in the home.

"The Respondent is a member of the Atlanta Braves baseball team. Although he is currently injured and not playing, he travels with the team. The team is in Los Angeles. Today, Monday, September 30, 1996, at approximately 9:30 A.M., Respondent again appeared at my home and demanded entry to the house allegedly to pick up some of his personal belongings. I was present and did not wish to see the Respondent. I arranged to have private security to come to the home, my agent came to the home, my attorney came to the home and the police were summoned. Respondent's personal belongings are *not* [emphasis added] at my home. All of his personal clothing and other items have been boxed and/or in the garage. There is absolutely no need whatsoever for Respondent to enter the house. He is more than welcome to have his personal belongings which are, as mentioned, in the garage.

"It was my further hope that Respondent would act like a gentlemen [*sic*], and arrange to come to the home at a mutually agreeable time to pick up his personal things. Unfortunately, Respondent did not see it that way. I personally heard the Respondent state to an unknown party on a cell phone if he is not given access to the home, he would 'break every one of the f'ing windows in the home and break the door down to get in because it was his home.'

"As a result of the intervention of the Los Angeles Police Department, Respondent entered the garage under police supervision and was allowed to remove his personal items. He did *not* [*sic*] take all of the items which were then available for him to take.

"I am in fear of my personal safety and wellbeing [*sic*]. I live in an area that is rather isolated and secluded and on a very narrow street. I do not have personal security with me at all times. The Respondent has kept guns in the home in the past and I do not know if there are any in the home which he left since our separation.

"There is absolutely no reason whatsoever that the Respondent should be allowed to come to my home for any reason. As indicated, I [am] more than willing to arrange a mutually agreeable time for Respondent to come to the home and remove the remaining personal items which he has there and which are already boxed and available for him to take.

"For all the foregoing reasons, I respectfully request that the Court order that Respondent stay at least 500 yards from my residence . . . at all times. For the record, I have no objections to those orders being made mutual in connection with our home in Atlanta."

Justice disputed Halle's version of the incident and asserted through a spokesman "I pose absolutely no threat to Halle." I got a look at the information in the Justice vs. Justice divorce file in 2002. The divorce was indeed a mud fight. Justice's lawyers pushed hard to depose actor Wesley Snipes, and Halle's lawyers filed several motions to short-circuit that push. Halle's lawyers also fought Justice's lawyers' motions seeking "any and all correspondence, memoranda, cards or any communication" between Halle and Spike Lee, Eddie Murphy, singer Christopher Williams, and others. In one document in the file, Halle is quoted as saying "I believe my husband, David Justice, is attempting to create a smear campaign." Halle's lawyers charged that Justice's lawyers are on "a fishing expedition . . . to support plaintiff's contention that she involves herself with certain men so that she may financially gain."

Perhaps the ugliest revelation in the file: Halle filed for divorce in California and had her husband served between the fifth and sixth innings of a Braves vs. Padres baseball game. She didn't even wait for the seventh inning stretch.

In the end, after the split, Halle was left with a nameless rage. Justice had seemed so perfect. He was handsome, smart, talented. He came from the same area, he had been raised in the same way. What had gone so horribly wrong? Halle said to *Essence* in 1996: "The day I filed for a divorce from David, I telephoned my father. I had to track him down because I hadn't talked with him in years. I was filled with pain and rage. I got him on the phone and unleashed all this anger. I released it. I told him how much he had hurt me by abandoning our family, by not being in my life when I was a child. At the end of the conversation, I think he said, 'I'm sorry.'

"I started therapy a year ago," Halle went on to say. "It took me a long time to identify my father as the source of my pain. I used to think that it didn't bother me that he wasn't around. Now I know that I missed a lot because he wasn't there for me."

After Justice, Halle came to the conclusion that marriage was harder than she thought. It was so hard, in fact, that it probably required two people to operate one properly. She felt as if she had been driving hers solo the entire time. Halle told the *Seattle Post-Intelligencer* in 1997: "Marriage is 100 times tough. You can make excuses why marriages don't work out. You can say it's careers. You can say whatever. But marriage takes two people who want the same things and who are willing to really compromise and take time to make it work."

Here's the simple take on Halle's romantic difficulties: She had a bad dad. And people often gravitate to someone like their parents. So she was in deep trouble even before she started. The problem is, when you're driven by a compulsion like that, you're usually the last person to know what's wrong. People don't want to believe that their past can drive them, because that robs them of free will. If Dad is the reason they're dating men that are bad for them, then, in a way, Dad is still in control—and for many folks that's too terrifying a thought to accept. So they ignore the source of their pain, pretend the root cause for the compulsion doesn't exist, and it leaves them even more powerless, like marionettes that can't see their own strings. "I always picked the wrong men," Halle told London's *Mirror* in 2001. "Not bad guys, just wrong for me. When I started to figure out who I was and chose men that offered me what I needed, instead of what I thought I wanted, it came together."

But before anything came together, Halle's life would have to completely fall apart.

"Hollywood is a strange place when you're in trouble.
Everyone is afraid it's contagious."

—JUDY GARLAND

"In my business, everybody lies to you.
They really like you if the movie you're in was
a success, and the minute you're in something
that bombs, you're on the 'out' list."

—HALLE BERRY

(Above) Halle in 1980, in eighth grade, as a member of the football and wrestling cheerleading squad of Heskett Junior High School, Bedford Heights, Ohio. (yearbookarchives. com) *(Below)* Halle in 1983 as a junior at Bedford High School, Bedford, Ohio. (yearbook-archives.com)

(Left) Halle in 1986 in the swimsuit competition in the Miss USA Pageant in Miami, Florida. (AP) *(Below)* Halle in 1986 finishing first runner-up at the Miss USA Pageant in Miami, Florida; Christy Fichtner of Texas, right, won. (AP)

(Above) Halle in 1993 with then-husband David Justice attending a discussion of violence and race relations at Banneker High School in Atlanta, Georgia. (AP)
(Below) Halle in 1996 with Kurt Russell promoting the movie *Executive Decision* in Las Vegas. (AP)

Halle in 2000 with Eric Benet at the premiere of the movie *X-Men* in New York. (AP)

(Above) Halle in 2000 at the 52nd Primetime Emmy Awards in Los Angeles with her Emmy for outstanding lead actress in a miniseries or movie for *Introducing Dorothy Dandridge.* (AP) *(Below)* Halle in 2001 with cast members from *Swordfish* at the movie's premiere in Los Angeles. From left, John Travolta, Halle, Hugh Jackman, and Don Cheadle. (AP)

(Above) Halle in 2002 at the 74th annual Academy Awards in Los Angeles winning the award for best actress. (AP)
(Opposite, top) Halle and her mother, Judith Berry, in 2002 at the 74th annual Academy Awards in Los Angeles. (AP)
(Opposite, bottom) Halle and Denzel Washington, who won the award for best actor, in 2002 at the 74th annual Academy Awards in Los Angeles. (AP)

Halle and co-star Pierce Brosnan in Cadiz, Spain, in 2002, where they were filming the James Bond movie *Die Another Day*. (AP/EFE)

FIVE

The Out List

This is the way she was going to die. He was gone now, she was sure of that. Whatever they had, if they ever had anything to begin with, had come to an end. She was a failure at relationships, just like she always was, just like her mother was, just like her father was. It was just all too difficult and she was all on her own here. So, it was decided. She would end it. She would collect her two dogs first. They were the only people who had ever stood by her, even though they weren't even people. In any case, she would take them with her. She would go into the garage and end it there, the two dogs with her. She would leave the car running and let the exhaust fill the garage, fill the interior of the car, fill her lungs. She would breathe it in deep. It would all be over soon. It would be for the best. She wondered what the papers would write. She hoped she'd at least make the papers. She'd accomplished enough for that hadn't she? The media would get it wrong anyway, they always did. She just hoped . . . she just hoped the dogs would understand.

A revolution doesn't begin until it stops. Once the fighting is done, and the new regime is in place, the battle truly commences: Will everything slide back into the status quo? Will the new boss be just like the old boss?

The black film revolution of the early nineties staged some spectacular battles—it grabbed magazine covers, it took hold of the public's attention, it spawned a slate of vibrant movies and spun out a galaxy of new stars.

But in a few short years it was all sucked away. This was the world into which Halle went job hunting:

- In 1987, one year after *She's Gotta Have It,* Sir Richard Attenborough's *Cry Freedom* told the story of South Africa's liberation struggle through the eyes of white newspaper editor Donald Woods, played by Kevin Kline (Denzel Washington, who played martyred South African activist Stephen Biko, was relegated to a smaller role).

- In 1988, director/actor Dennis Hopper's *Colors* explored the world of Los Angeles street gangs, but told its story through the eyes of two LAPD cops, played by Sean Penn and Robert Duvall.

- Also in 1988, Alan Parker's Oscar-winning *Mississippi Burning,* a dramatic film about the FBI's fight against the Klan and its crusade to bring the murderers of three civil rights workers to justice in the 1960s was released. In truth, the FBI did not play the kind of relentless heroic role portrayed in the film. Even worse, the real heroes of the story—black civil rights workers—are relegated to the background and are depicted as victims waiting for the G-men to save them.

- In 1996, director Joel Schumacher brought to the big screen the John Grisham novel *A Time to Kill,* starring then-newcomer Matthew McConaughey in the lead with then-veteran Samuel L. Jackson in a supporting part. The film told the story of a young white lawyer in Mississippi (McConaughey) and all the strife he and his family endure for going to bat for a black murder client (Jackson). Once again, prime black talent was being used to tell a story about racism in which whites, not blacks, were the protagonists and the sufferers.

- Also in 1996, director Robert Altman, the maverick director behind *M*A*S*H* and *Nashville,* made a movie called *Kansas City,* set during the height of that city's jazz renaissance. Not one of the main characters in the film was black, except for Harry Belafonte in a smallish part. Years earlier, Francis Ford Coppola, the masterful director of *The Godfather,* pulled much the same stunt with his movie *The Cotton Club* (1984). Set during the Harlem renaissance in 1928, the film's focus is on a white jazzman, played by Richard Gere. Gregory Hines does some tap dancing as the second lead, but the African-American story line takes a backseat.

This was the atmosphere in which Halle was trying to polish her freshly minted stardom. And there was much weighing on her mind beyond work—chiefly, her recent divorce. She tried, as much as she could, to focus on the positive. "When you go through bad times you find what your capacity to learn is," Halle told the *Cleveland Plain Dealer* in 1999. She also had a new worry: For the first time her thespian clock was ticking. Hollywood was always looking for the next sweet young thing. Once you hit thirty in Tinseltown you could still be sweet, but you sure weren't young and you definitely weren't next. "I had a lot of anxiety about turning 30," Halle told *Ebony* in 1999. "I was divorcing at the time and I felt like such a failure. I wanted a family desperately and, being diabetic, I thought, 'I'm not going to get to have babies because by the time I heal, I'm going to be too old.'"

Through the years, over her short career, the lost opportunities, the parts just missed, the major movies that had just slipped out of her grasp, had been piling up. Throughout her career, she had sold herself short on occasion, because otherwise nothing would be selling at all—so she took smaller roles in films such as the limp college football drama *The Program* (1993) and the critically panned action comedy *Father Hood* (1993). All along Halle dreamed of getting the parts she saw going to Winona Ryder and Julia Roberts and Marisa Tomei. She auditioned for *The Silence of the Lambs* (1991), but didn't get a part. She wanted a role in *Point of No Return* (1993), the American remake of the French hit *La Femme Nikita,* but couldn't even get a meeting with the director, John Badham (Bridget Fonda nabbed the lead).

She put herself up for *Indecent Proposal*—a movie about a woman who, with her husband's backing, sells a single night of sex for one million dollars—but a producer for the movie, according to Halle, didn't want to "go black" with the role because of the risk of offending minorities. She went out for the Tom Cruise legal thriller *The Firm*—she wanted to grab the small part of a woman who seduces Cruise on a beach just to prove she could do it, that audiences would accept race-neutral casting, but she lost out again. (Interestingly enough, Cruise would be paired up with a black love interest, Thandie Newton, in *Mission Impossible 2* in 2000.) Halle tried out for *Intersection* (1994) but came up with nothing (Sharon Stone and Lolita Davidovich were cast instead).

The misses just kept on coming. So when two movies came up that offered her the chance to have her name, and her name alone, above the title, she jumped at the chances. Actors get their name above the title alone all the time; actresses have to fight for it, and sometimes they pay dearly for it, in terms of quality. They're willing to do low-quality projects just for that perk of being a solo headliner. It's often a Faustian bargain that burns loyal fans. Just ask anyone who saw Jennifer Lopez in *Angel Eyes* (2001) and *Enough* (2002)—if you can find anyone who actually sat through them.

The first film Halle headlined solo was the low-budget family film *Race the Sun* (1996). It's a film that belongs to a peculiar subgenre best called "Hero Teacher Movies." Typically, Hero Teacher Movies come in five varieties:

1. The Dead Teacher. Here, a film looks back fondly on some special instructor who usually buys it before the end. Good examples are *Goodbye, Mr. Chips* (1939), a film about a British schoolmaster looking back, and *October Sky* (1999), a terrifically moving and criminally overlooked film about a teacher (Laura Dern) who inspires her kids to get out of their dead-end mining town.

2. The Sexy Teacher. These teachers are good at what they do and wind up in bed with fellow teachers or students. There's the fine comedy *Rushmore* (1998) and *Bright Road* (1953), about a teacher (the luminous Dorothy Dandridge) in a small southern town (Harry Belafonte, who plays her principal, is the love interest).

3. The Rebel Teacher. *Dead Poets Society* (1989) with Robin Williams shaking up a prep school; *To Sir, With Love* (1967) with Sidney Poitier, in which he tries, against the odds, to educate a group of rowdy, mostly white students in London (interesting aside: in the original book version, he has an affair with a white teacher), and *Not One Less* (1999), a fine Chinese film by the great director Yang Zimou about a thirteen-year-old girl, barely older than her students, who is forced by circumstances to take over her class.

4. The Great White Teacher. *Dangerous Minds* (1995), in which Michelle Pfeiffer plays a teacher

trying to educate mostly minority kids with a stiff black administrator, Courtney B. Vance, getting in her way, and *Music of the Heart* (1999), in which Meryl Streep plays a music teacher trying to educate mostly minority kids, with a stiff black administrator, played by Angela Bassett (coincidentally, Vance's real-life spouse), getting in her way. Other examples include *The King and I* (1956) and *The Blackboard Jungle* (1955). (Interesting aside: the Hispanic actor Andy Garcia filmed a role as Pfeiffer's love interest in *Dangerous Minds,* but he was entirely cut out of the movie.)

5. The Crazy Minority Teacher. *Stand and Deliver* (1987) and *Lean on Me* (1989). The message of both these films is nurturing fails, tough love works, and conservative minorities get the job done. Whether you buy that message is up to you.

So, given this context, *Race the Sun,* though dramatically weak, is something of a genre breakthrough. Halle plays a teacher who inspires a group of low-esteem Hawaiian kids to build a solar car and enter a contest in Australia. Halle has rarely looked better than she did in this movie; she doesn't dress glamorously (she is playing a schoolteacher) and so her inner beauty is really allowed to shine. She's a minority teacher who motivates her kids not with a bat or with tough love but by getting them to trust in themselves. The film would have been better if it had relied more on the local flavor—there's little here about the culture of the Hawaiian kids. Still, *Race the Sun* is an okay film for kids. And the film's first race sequence, in which the kids go up against the rich preppies, is staged with some verve.

The next film Halle got to headline solo was *The Rich Man's Wife*. This film, to paraphrase a character from the movie *Ghost World*, is one of those films that's so bad it's almost good, but then it loops back to bad again. Halle told the *Sun Reporter* in 1996: "There aren't many scripts that have a strong central female character as the driving force of the movie, and it gave me something new to do, and an opportunity to be the leading lady. . . . This movie allowed me to do something different from other roles I've played. It's a murder mystery, film noir kind of movie, which I've wanted to do for a long time." She went on to confide that hand in hand with opportunity came anxiety: "It's satisfying but I'm also scared to death! I'd be lying if I said that I didn't feel pressure, but I also know why I'm doing what I'm doing, and I'm really doing this because I love to act. And I love to be in front of the camera. It's what I get the most pleasure from."

Halle told host Mark McEwen on *CBS This Morning* in 1996 that when she first got the script for the movie she was excited, but somewhat suspicious. "Well, I thought honestly, 'They're offering it to me—what's wrong with it?'" Halle said. "It's not often that I just get offered good scripts." One deciding factor: She wanted to work with a female director, and the film was written and directed by

Amy Holden Jones, who was also the screenwriter for the film that helped launch Julia Roberts, *Mystic Pizza,* as well as the Robert Redford/Demi Moore hit that Halle got rejected for, *Indecent Proposal.* With a screenwriter/director with credentials like that signing on to *The Rich Man's Wife* it seemed like a pretty good risk to take. "As women we connected in a certain way that men just don't," Halle said. "Sometimes the communication was nonverbal, because as women we just got it."

I talked to Amy Holden Jones in 2002 about her work with Halle. Jones said: "I'm friends with [director] Stephen Gyllenhaal, so I had seen her work in *Losing Isaiah,* and I thought she really did a great job in it. It was made for Joe Roth when he was interested in making thrillers or genre movies without, at the time, huge stars. Halle was not a huge star at that time, she was breaking in as opposed to being established as she is now. She seemed like a great choice, and I ran it by them, and [producer] Roger Birnbaum felt it was a great idea and we went to her and she wanted to do it. It was a pretty clear choice right from the beginning."

The plot is this: Josie Potenza (Halle) is trapped in a loveless marriage to a wealthy TV executive (Christopher McDonald) who is also having an affair. Meanwhile, Halle is having an affair of her own with a sexy young Englishman, played by Clive Owen, who would later garner critical acclaim in *Croupier, Gosford Park,* and *The Bourne Identity.* Halle runs into a drifter (Peter Greene) who kills her husband and then blackmails her: If she doesn't pay up, he'll tell the cops she planned the whole thing. There are some fairly intriguing *Usual Suspects*–like twists and turns near the end, but it's too late to save the movie. Very few films, like *The Sixth Sense* and *The Others,* can pull off the trick of giving you an ending so surprising that it makes you reassess what you've been watching for the last two hours and enjoy it even more. The moviegoer wants to feel as if he or she could have figured out the ending, even if he or she didn't. If the climax appears to be pulled out of a hat, it feels like a fraud. Unless the final twist seems earned, unless the final ending seems inevitable and logical but diabolically clever, a trick-ending film leaves the moviegoer feeling cheated. Why couldn't the screenwriter display such wit before the movie ended?

Jones, in my talk with her, has fond memories of Halle's working style, but not so fond memories of one of her co-stars. Jones told me: "Of course, she's stunningly beautiful. But the first day of shooting, what was probably most impressive, was how spectacularly well prepared she was. How professional she was, how meticulous she was. She still remains one of the hardest working, most professional actresses I've ever worked with. I think you might expect a diva of some kind with that much beauty. But she was every inch the hardworking professional trying to get the movie to be as good as it could possibly be. I don't think there was ever a single moment when she wasn't there on time, wasn't prepared. And it was a difficult picture for her in many ways. It was a hard point in her life. She was beginning to have problems with David Justice, and Peter Greene was quite difficult to work with for all of us, but Halle was right face-to-face with him all the time in the scenes with him where he's playing a violent character threatening her. It was certainly the hardest on her."

"[Greene was] an extreme method actor. He became very volatile whenever the camera was rolling. Such that occasionally Halle was actually physically afraid of him. In a scene in which he was going to get rough, you always had to worry whether he was going to get too rough. Unlike Halle, he really was a prima donna. So here we have someone with less of a reputation and less of a name, luckier to get the part, who was constantly demanding more attention, time, care, to get him on the spot doing what he was supposed to do, than Halle who was always right there, doing anything she could. It really wasn't terribly fair to her."

Halle was also going through some difficulties at the time—physical and emotional. Said Jones: "It was a very vigorous shoot. She had health issues that required her to really rest when she was not working and prescribed a little bit the hours she should work. So you had to be pretty sensitive about her privacy for those reasons. She really has to take care of herself to feel her best."

The breakup of her marriage to Justice, which was taking place during the filming, probably took a toll, but Halle worked hard not to show it. Jones told me: "I really only realized that it was difficult later. She and David obviously loved each other. He came to the set several times. I was in her trailer when he hit a home run that won a game in the World Series and she was so excited. They were such an extraordinarily beautiful couple. And he's a fascinating man, extraordinarily interesting to talk to. At the time I simply thought how wonderful that these two amazing people have each other. But you also always had to wonder how they could deal with so much separation. They were quite private about it—as far as I could tell they were dealing with it. It was only after they broke up that I realized she'd been coping with this stuff herself, behind the scenes."

The Rich Man's Wife was a box-office flop, pulling in only $8,538,000 domestically. Clive Owen, one of Halle's co-stars revealed later that he wasn't too happy with the final cinematic product. In 2001 he told *USA Today:* "I did that film because I wanted to come to America and shoot a movie there. . . . I would never again take a film for that reason."

Minority actors, however, are often faced with limited choices: pimps and prostitutes, movies with thin scripts and low budgets, projects with tight shooting schedules and minimum pay. As Robert Townsend famously declared in his Tinseltown send-up *Hollywood Shuffle,* "There's always work at the post office," but for actors who haven't worked in a while, it's very tempting to rationalize taking a substandard part. After Angela Bassett was nominated for an Oscar for her fiery performance as Tina Turner in *What's Love Got to Do With It* (1993), she thought job offers would pour in. But she was still a black woman in Hollywood and she didn't work for a year. Halle found that she was going through similar problems. She is a tenacious pursuer of quality parts, but she was nonetheless turned down for role after role—and sometimes she had to grit her teeth and see parts that she had fought for, that she was right for, go to lesser-known, less-talented nonminority actresses. Halle told *The Express* in 2002: "When there is a love story with a really high-profile male star, the directors will say, 'Oh, we love Halle, we just don't want to go black with this part.'"

It's a dilemma with roots in old Hollywood. On October 22, 1938, Ruby Berkley Goodwin, a writer for the *Pittsburgh Courier*, an African-American newspaper, wrote a story in which she challenged her readers to join a letter-writing campaign to persuade film studios to create better roles for blacks. In her article, she quoted Al Cohen, the head of Christie Productions, who told her that other moviegoers were making their voices heard: "We have received many letters from southern white people who complain that we dress our Negro players too fine, that they talk too proper," Cohen said. "We'd honestly like to know what Negro fans think of the pictures we produce."

But the problem persisted. Apparently, very few letters from blacks came in following the original *Pittsburgh Courier* piece, and later on, Goodwin chastised her readers. She wrote: "We must face facts! Hollywood is in business to make money through entertainment . . . it is so much easier to blame Hollywood for ignoring us than it is to blame ourselves for not making Hollywood conscious of the vast army of Negro fans and their appreciation of Negro players. Get that cramp out of your arm and write a letter . . . to Hattie McDaniel and tell her she was a riot in *Shopworn Angel.* Talk to Hollywood in the language they understand—fan mail—and Hollywood will talk back to you by putting more Negro players in super productions." (McDaniel, the first black performer to win an Oscar—a best supporting actress award in 1939 for her role as Mammy in *Gone With the Wind*—had her own struggles with Hollywood. According to the book *Inside Oscar* by Mason Wiley and Damien Bona, the night of her big win, McDaniel and her escort were seated at an isolated table for two at the very rear of the Coconut Grove, the venue where the Oscars were handed out.)

Still the problem persisted. Shortly after World War II, Betsy Blair, wife of Screen Actors Guild board member Gene Kelly, proposed a resolution that was passed by the SAG membership in the fall of 1946 by a margin of 992 in favor and 34 opposed. The measure read:

> *WHEREAS, Negro actors have a long and honorable history in American theatre and in the motion picture industry and played an important part in the formation of our Guild, and*
> *WHEREAS, unemployment among our Negro Guild members has reached a point more alarming than at any time in Guild history, and*
> *WHEREAS, Negro parts are being omitted from a great many screenplays and are, in many cases, actu-*

ally being cut out of books and plays when adapted to the screen, and

WHEREAS, in several instances producers have even gone to the length of using white actors in Negro roles,

NOW, THEREFORE, BE IT RESOLVED that the Screen Actors Guild use all of its power to oppose discrimination against Negroes in the motion picture industry, and

BE IT FURTHER RESOLVED that a special committee be set up at once to implement this policy and to meet with representatives of the Screen Writers' Guild and the Screen Directors' Guild and the Motion Picture Producers Association in order to establish in the industry a policy of presenting Negro characters on the screen in the true relation they bear to American life.

As a result of the resolution, an Anti-Discrimination Committee was formed in November 1946, but it was promptly dissolved at a SAG board meeting on March 10, 1947—the same meeting at which Ronald Reagan (yes, *that* Ronald Reagan) was elected to the post of SAG president for the first time, thus beginning his career in elective office.

More than a half century later, the problem persists. With few women, and almost no minorities, calling the shots in Hollywood, women and minorities often tend to get overlooked in terms of casting and script development. The major filmmaking guilds (actors, directors, producers, and writers) are 80 to 90 percent white. Only about 10 percent of the board members or partners on the biggest talent agencies are women and there are, at the time of this writing, no minorities. There is no minority in Hollywood, at the time of this writing, with the power to green-light a major movie. That means if you want to get a black movie made, a white executive has to okay it—and that executive is in most cases going to be male.

Hollywood isn't changing, but America is. America is getting browner, America is eating spicier food, America is bouncing to hip-hop, grooving to salsa, and turning Mandarin-language, English-subtitled films like *Crouching Tiger, Hidden Dragon* into $100 million hits. And yet offerings like *Crouching Tiger,* despite that film's runaway success, are few and far between. Hollywood seems to dismiss every minority success as a fluke and refuses, for the most part, to replicate it. So even as Jennifer Lopez pulls them in at the box office, Hollywood drags its heels in releasing more films like *Selena, Mi Familia,* and *La Bamba* (all profitable releases).

Minority actors often find themselves with two choices: Either they can do the "Hollywood Shuffle" and play ultrastereotypical parts just to get work, or they can play homogenized parts just to get work. Angela Bassett's first screen credit prior to getting her first meaty role in *Boyz N the Hood* was as an unnamed "Prostitute at Headquarters" in the TV movie *Doubletake.* This for a woman who studied at Yale School of Drama. On the other end of the spectrum, Jennifer Lopez's films since she became a star have been deracinated—she mostly plays opposite non-Latino whites, and in the comedy *The Wedding Planner* she played an Italian. Certainly actors should play a range of roles and not be hemmed in, but one wonders if Lopez's career will continue to blossom if it's cut off from its roots.

For her part, Halle longed for casting agents and directors and studio executives to see her without their race goggles on. "I wish I could have played in *Pretty Woman* so I could be [actress] Julia Roberts right now," Halle said to the *Atlanta Journal-Constitution*. "But that happens with a lot of the roles that I've tried to be seen for, the common comeback is always, 'Well, she's black.' Okay, well, I know that, tell me something else. Then they're like, 'Well, that's gonna change the whole effect of the movie because we have a white guy that's supposed to be your brother and that just isn't going to work.'"

So Berry tried to suck it up and soldier on. "I always have to rise above it," Halle told the *New York Times* in 2002. "I can't go off like a raving lunatic even though my heart wants me to. I say, 'Okay, take a deep breath,' and I realize that's the insidiousness of racism. People don't even know when they're being racist."

All of which brings us to *B.A.P.S.* (1997). Townsend, the director who bears culpability for this disastrous uncomedy, seems to have forgotten, for a moment, the phrase that he coined, "There's always work at the post office." Surely working for UPS or FedEx or even Mail Boxes

Etc. would have been preferable to putting out this mess of a movie. *B.A.P.S.* (the title is an acronym for "Black American Princesses") is about two round-the-way girls (Halle and newcomer Natalie Desselle) with long, curled nails, big gold earrings, and gold teeth who set off to land a part in a Heavy D video and end up hooking up with an ailing billionaire (played by Martin Landau, in his most ridiculous role since *Space: 1999*). Halle, in another tribute to her talent, never seems to play down to her character; she works hard to make this film funny and moving, even though it is neither.

B.A.P.S. was a minor disappointment at the box office; it didn't cost much to make, but it didn't pull in much either, drawing only $7,240,000 at the box office.

It's hard to understand why *B.A.P.S.* was made in the first place. Perhaps Halle made *B.A.P.S.* because she needed a big stupid laugh; perhaps she needed to make a comedy full of laughs that would take her away from her life, which was marked by the absence of laughter. One day, during the shooting of *B.A.P.S.*, Townsend got into an argument with a crew member who was brazenly reading a tabloid with Halle on the cover—right in front of Halle's trailer. It was around this time, in the wake of her split with David Justice, that Halle contemplated suicide. Halle told Barbara Walters in 2002: "Well, I think I was still using men and my mate to identify who I was. And when that was gone, then I was nothing."

Happily, common sense stepped in, and she put the

plan to the side. Halle said: "It's almost like I had a flash of you know that good angel and the bad angel on my shoulder. . . . And something was telling me on the right side of my brain, girl don't do it, girl don't do it. Think of your mother . . . I couldn't do that to her. So I got out."

Halle, judged so often by her skin—how beautiful it was to some, how ugly it was to others, how dark it was to some, how light it was to others—simply developed a tougher hide. Said Halle to *Ebony* in 1999: "There was a time after the divorce when I was really bitter. I convinced myself I didn't want to get married again and that was okay because I didn't need to rush into another relationship. Now that I'm stronger and wiser, I know what I need in a relationship. I know what it looks like and what it feels like. I know what I want in a man."

And what did she want? "Someone who values the institution of marriage and all that means. It's one thing to be out with the cameras flashing and the fans waving, but I need someone who I can share the quiet moments with. Someone who can be happy sitting on the sofa with me, just looking at the sunset and have that be enough."

Would Halle ever get her wish?

"Marriage is too interesting an experience
to be tried only once."
—Eva Gabor

"In my history with men, when I show
signs of not being the beauty queen
they signed up to date, they split."
—Halle Berry

SIX

Eric Benet

She shouldn't be here. Not in this place at this particular time at night. She was just outside the Beverly Center in Los Angeles. She was in the parking garage, walking toward her car. The mall was closing and she was loaded down with bags full of things she had just bought. She got this feeling there was someone behind her, she didn't know who, but there was a presence. She turned around, but she couldn't see anyone. She kept walking, perhaps a little quicker now, maybe a little more scared now, almost certainly aware of the fact that the time was late and she was alone and she really shouldn't be here, not at this place at this particular time of night. She was at her car now, she had to get her keys ready, but now she felt something at her back, perhaps felt some breathing against her neck. Somebody was sticking something against her spine— a gun, a knife—she didn't know what. This was a robbery, she knew that now. She felt that sickly scared feeling in her stomach, that clammy feeling on her

• 139 •

brow. She gave him everything—her purse, her jew-
elry. She wanted to give him her car. She just wanted
it over. She just wanted it done. She had already been
through so much. And then it was over.

Halle Berry has a recurring dream. She is talking, saying something, having a conversation of some sort, and suddenly all her teeth fly out of her mouth. She is left there, toothless, without molars or canines, without a smile or the means to produce one. She can't speak anymore, she can't produce words. She is silent, muted, without a voice. She has thought about this dream and wondered what it means, but she hasn't found the answer. She thought the dream would end, perhaps she believed that with success, the symbols, whatever their meaning, would lose their force, let go of their grip on her subconscious. Perhaps she thought, with happier times, she would have happier dreams, ones that were less provocative, less cryptic. But she keeps having the same dream. And her teeth keep flying out of her mouth. And she stands there voiceless.

Her marriage to David Justice had left a mark, spiritually, emotionally, physically. When they were together, she had had his first name tattooed on her back. That was a mistake. *Hollywood Rule No. 256: Never tattoo the name of another celebrity anywhere on one's body.* Now the marriage was over, and he was still there. He was literally behind her yet always with her.

Everything was in doubt now. She was questioning her worth as an actress, her value as a woman. She had been ready to give up her profession for him, and now her career was all she had left. She had been contemplating suicide, she was troubled by bad dreams, and, around that time, to add insult to injury, she was mugged in the parking garage of the Beverly Center. Her assailant, whoever he or she was, came up behind her and stuck something in her back. He or she made off with Halle's purse, her bags, her jewelry, and something even more precious—her sense of safety. She seemed to have no haven now. Her whole life seemed under siege.

Halle and Eric Benet met sometime in 1997. How they met and where they met depend on who you ask. After, in her eyes, being burned by the media during her relationship with Justice, Halle was a little more secretive when it came to Benet. Yes, she discussed him in the press, and, okay, they would venture out in public together to awards shows, movie openings, and concerts, but the details of their relationship were obscured.

Halle's version of the way they met goes something like this: "I met him through a friend and she introduced us," Halle told the *Mirror* in 2001. "We became mates and talked on the Internet a lot. There weren't any sparks or that mad passionate attraction in the beginning. Then one day I turned to him and said, 'You know what? I think I love you.' Eric's a very earthy, spiritual guy. I was also a fan of his music, so that helped. I've been on that rise before, thinking, 'Oh, he's the one,' and then a year later, I've realized he's not."

His version is a little different: Benet told the

Milwaukee Journal Sentinel in 2001 that "We used to go to the same L.A. mall, and she'd often come up and say hi. From there, we just began hanging out, and before you know it, we were an item. Or make that 'she' was the item. I was just the guy that the press would refer to as 'Berry and her escort, an aspiring R and B singer' . . . it was weird at first. Here I was used to getting most of the attention in whatever scene I happened to be involved in. But now I was dating a woman whose profile was 10 times bigger."

It was not, at least relative to her relationship with Justice, a whirlwind courtship. Halle had made the first moves with Justice—giving him her phone number, asking him to marry her, cutting through the usual delays. She decided to take a different approach this time around. Every failed relationship is like a weight. They make you stronger, they build up your endurance, but they eventually weigh you down, make you move slower, and sometimes they make you pull a muscle. A few failures put you into game-shape, you're ready for the world, to meet your true match; too many failures immobilize you, leave you imprisoned under the weight of defeat. Halle told AP Online in March 2002: "I took the time to become his friend, get to know him and also have him get to know me, the real me, not the image of me."

After the end of a marriage, or after the demise of a long relationship, it's hard not to see the reflection of one's ex in the eyes of one's current flame. Everything they do, at first at least, is either not like the ex or exactly like the ex. Nobody wants to make the same mistake twice. We'd all rather we didn't make the same mistake even once, for that matter.

David Justice was a big star when he hooked up with Halle, even bigger than she was. Benet was a small star when he hooked up with Halle, much smaller than she was. Eric Benet Jordan was born in Milwaukee, Wisconsin, in 1970. His middle name was inspired by the poet Stephen Vincent Benet (1898–1943); Stephen Vincent Benet was the author of "John Brown's Body," a long narrative poem of the Civil War, and the short story "The Devil and Daniel Webster." Unlike David Justice, and unlike Halle, Eric had a large, loving family, and two parents he was very close to. Eric's father was a police officer, who was a fan of classical music, his mother was a fan of singing around the house, and his sister Lisa (one of his four siblings, all older) was a fan of R and B. So he grew up in a house that was filled with music and vocalizing.

Although Eric was born in a black section of town, he was transferred, at a young age, to an all-white grade school on the West Side of Milwaukee. The experience broadened his tastes and made him more receptive to different ideas and cultures and points of view. Eric said: "I'd make friends with all sorts of kids: black, white, and Asian. But back in my neighborhood, people would see me with friends from school—some white or Asian—and be like, 'Um, what's this about?'" Eric eventually started a series of bands, trying to find an audience for his eclectic take on R and B. His first band, which featured his cousin George Nash Jr. and his sister Lisa, he called Gerard. His next band, which also featured his cousin George and his sister Lisa, he called Benet. The band was signed to EMI in 1990, and the group's self-titled debut album was released in 1992. Eric favored a sound that was both new and old, one that drew from the classic soul of the past—Marvin Gaye, Stevie Wonder, Donny Hathaway—but also tried to move soul into the future. Critics saw him as part of the neo-soul movement of the nineties, along with Erykah Badu, D'Angelo, Maxwell, and other R and B innovators. Benet's debut, however, didn't attract the notice that folks like Badu were generating—*Benet* sold only seventy thousand copies and didn't even go gold. The act generated some positive buzz, however, and Eric and his sister were optimistic that they'd find their niche and catch on. Benet felt the industry was controlled by suits, and good music was getting strangled. He told the *Sun Reporter* in 2001: "It's very much controlled by corporate America . . . the biggest problem is it's a creative industry controlled by noncreative people, it's not conducive to creativity. It's weird. There are narrow confines of music and if you step outside those confines they don't know how to categorize you so you don't get any [radio] airplay."

Around 1992 tragedy struck—and it came in threes. Over the course of about eighteen months, Eric lost his record deal; he lost his father to cancer; and his ex-girlfriend Tami Stauff (with whom he had a daughter, India, in 1992) died in a car wreck. Tami lingered in a coma for five days before dying. Benet went into a slow shock, dropping out of entertainment except for the odd songwriting gig. He took in his daughter and got a job at UPS. He told *The Independent* (London) in 1999: "It was really the hardest thing I've ever gone through. Even losing my father, as traumatic as that was, didn't hurt as much because . . . we at least knew he was dying; we all—my mom, my two sisters, my brother—got the chance to say goodbye. Tami and I weren't actually together at the time she died—I was seeing India every weekend—but the feelings of guilt, remorse, bereavement, depression just took over. Hearing India call my name when I came home from work at the end of the day felt like all I had to hang on to."

In 1996, as neo-soul caught fire on the charts, Benet signed with Warner Bros. and reemerged with his first solo album, titled *True to Myself.* One of the songs of that CD, "While You Were Here," dealt with his feelings in the wake of his ex-girlfriend's death. The album sold a solid 500,000 copies and went gold. In 1999, Benet released *A Day in the Life,* with guest appearances from R and B diva Faith Evans and bassist/rapper/singer Me'Shell Ndegeocello. That release sold a million copies and went platinum. But Benet wanted even bigger and better things. A million copies is nice, but it doesn't make you a superstar, not with what labels have to pay to promote new acts, and not with tot-pop acts like 'NSync and Eminem and Britney Spears selling a million copies in a week, as they were around that period. Benet told the *Milwaukee Journal Sentinel* in 2001: "All this kiddie R and B teen-pop stuff out there today? I look at R and B and think, there can't be a top without a bottom. There are always cycles in the music industry of crap that gets pushed and sells a lot. . . . After awhile, the audience gets fed up, and its response creates a demand for a cycle of good music."

Benet wasn't at the top of the music charts, but he was already a hit with his new girlfriend. Halle and Benet became engaged in 1999. Halle told *Movieline* in 2001: "I've met some pretty intelligent men, but what would make a man amazing to me is somebody who could love me unconditionally. I always wanted a father in my life, never having had one. Eric is amazing because he loves me no matter what—when I fuck up, when I'm less than perfect. In my history with men, when I show signs of being not the beauty queen they signed up to date, they split. But Eric loves me with all my flaws and inconsistencies and double standards. He says that's what he loves about me."

She was ready to move ahead with a new relationship because she thought she had the mistake of the past figured out. "There's a reason the first marriage didn't work," Halle told the *Los Angeles Times* in 2002. "But I learned so much through the process about myself. I think this time around I was better able to choose a better mate for myself. I understand better what I need and was able to choose a partner who was more compatible. Still, I was a little skeptical. We dated for quite awhile this time."

David Justice was history. Halle had her old tattoo, the

one of David's name on her back, colored over and turned into a sunflower. It was symbolic for her. Sunflowers closed up when it was dark, and turned inward to regenerate. They also opened up when it was sunny and followed the light. She wanted to be like that. She wanted to color over the mistakes of the past, regenerate, and follow the sun. Benet, to her, was like daylight through a picture window.

So, in February 2001 there was another wedding. Halle and Eric decided to tie the knot two weeks before the ceremony took place. They did it with the blessing of Halle's mother, Judith, who told one interviewer: "I love Eric. He's so grounded, so spiritual, so compassionate." The media, at the time, didn't know the location of the nuptials: a California beach. The wedding announcements were messages in bottles. The note inside read: "To have life we were chosen by love to share eternal love we've chosen each other. Introducing Mr. and Mrs. Eric Benet Jordan." Eric wore a white silk suit; Halle wore a simple Ristarose dress. For their honeymoon, the newlyweds spent two weeks on one of the Maldive islands in the Indian Ocean.

After the wedding Halle began to long for motherhood. She told *Ebony* in 2000: "I became very maternal almost in that moment. I didn't just want a child. I wanted his child. Our child. Not long after we get married, that will be one of the first things on our agenda." She soon took India for her own, telling reporters that she considered herself to be the girl's mother. Halle told *Ebony:* "People say to me, 'Oh she's so lucky to have you in her life. Well, I'm the lucky one. India sees me as unstoppable and when I'm with her, I feel that." Her close friends took note of Halle's new relationship. "They're very close," Yvonne Sims, Halle's longtime friend, said to *People*. "It's quality time she spends with her, shopping, talking, dealing with mother-daughter stuff."

Halle seemed to put aside, at least for the time being, the wish to bear a child herself. "If time doesn't run out for me, it will happen when it happens," she told *USA Today* in 2002. "And if it doesn't, and we've talked about it, having India has totally fulfilled that maternal need. You don't have to have a baby from your very own body to be a mother and have that need fulfilled."

While dating Eric, Halle signed up for what she thought could be the role of her career. It was in the political satire *Bulworth* and it was opposite Warren Beatty. Berry had a meeting with him and was very impressed. He was a genuine Hollywood legend; he knew what is was to be a sex symbol, and he knew what it was to have longevity. Beatty had a strong track record; he had won rave reviews and Oscars, and he had legions of fans and a reputation for creative daring. An actor is lucky if he or she makes one genuinely classic movie over the course of a career; Beatty had made a handful, including *Splendor in the Grass, Bonnie and Clyde, Shampoo, Heaven Can Wait*, and *Reds*.

Bulworth is a semi-noble failure, one that tries to pay tribute to the insurgent spirit of African-American culture by co-opting it and creating a story in which an older white man seems to understand the needs and goals of black culture more than blacks themselves do. The movie's plot is this: Jay Billington Bulworth (Warren Beatty) is a Democratic senator from California who has sold out his liberal values in order to raise funds. Disillusioned and suicidal, he takes out a large life insurance policy on himself and hires a hit man to end his own life. Driven half-crazy by his desperate actions, he begins to speak in hip-hop slang and rhyme and soon he and others realize he's channeling the true values of America. Halle Berry plays a street-smart woman from Compton who Bulworth falls for; it turns out she's actually been hired to help assassinate him. In the end, though, she decides against betraying him and, before giving him a love-drenched kiss, she tells him "You're my nigga."

Bulworth has some nice moments—Beatty's senatorial raps, though they lack the dexterous rhythms of true hip-hop, contain some biting truths about the way money, more than people, drives today's politics. When Bulworth goes on a national TV show and declares "Rich people have always stayed on top—by dividing white people from colored people," the movie comes to a kind of anarchic life. Bulworth goes on to say: "All we need is a voluntary free-spirited program of racial deconstruction. Everybody's just got to keep fucking everybody till we're all the same color." It's a naive statement—one can imagine Beatty using a version of it as a pickup line to Berry—have sex with me and eventually it will help desegregate the schools!—but nonetheless the line has a sort of impish, populist charm.

But beneath the hip-hop bravado, *Bulworth* doesn't really respect its black characters. None of them are developed and all are stereotypes. Halle's family is right out of a right-wing fantasy vision of life in the 'hood: dozens of kids all crowded into a tiny housing unit. Beatty's clichéd take on the 'hood also includes drug dealing, heat-packing grade-schoolers who only need ice cream to sooth their street rage. Halle does some fine acting with her eyes—with a series of looks she goes from sexually intrigued to murderous to genuinely emotionally attached. But we learn little about her back story and what her hopes, dreams, and fears really are. *Bulworth* merely borrows signifiers from black culture and never gives anything back. In later years, Eminem would do much the same thing—his music is driven by rhythms associated primarily with black artists, but his lyrics are really only meant for white listeners (on one song, "White America," he even addresses them directly, as if no black people could possibly be listening). Unlike Beatty's *Bulworth*, Eminem's brand of rap has almost no political content whatsoever. It's drive-by hip-hop.

Halle's character in *Bulworth* conforms to another long-standing stereotype in the movies: the African American as betrayer. Halle played one earlier in her career in *The Flintstones,* where she portrayed a secretary who was set to betray, of all people, Fred Flintstone, before she has a change of heart. In *The Empire Strikes Back* (1980), Lando Calrissian (Billy Dee Williams) betrays Luke Skywalker, Han Solo, and Princess Leia to

Darth Vader and the rebellion, before he changes his mind and joins the rebellion (*Empire*, despite this plot point, is still a terrific film). In *Total Recall* (1990), Arnold Schwarzenegger is betrayed by a jive-talking, dreadlocked cabdriver. And in the movie version of *Jesus Christ Superstar* (1973) the patron antisaint of all betrayers, Judas Iscariot, is played by a black actor (singer Carl Anderson, who turns in a brilliant performance). The signal from Hollywood seems to be this: Don't trust black folks, especially the ones that seem to be your friends. Luke Skywalker, Schwarzenegger, and Jesus did it and look what happened to them. This anxiety gets a lot of attention from Hollywood screenwriters in part because very few of them are black. Traitor characters also allow mainstream filmmakers to avoid protests over content: full-out black villains, especially in the wake of the black film revolution, can be controversial. Black traitor characters straddle the line—for part of the film at least, they are on the side of the heroes.

Berry was surprised by the hostile reaction *Bulworth* received in the black press. Halle told *GQ* in July 1999: "I thought black people would applaud this effort. But so many black people got offended by the movie or felt it aided in their oppression. I was baffled. My response was, lighten up and look at the message and don't get caught up in the stereotypes."

Bulworth, which got rave reviews and even some Oscar buzz, was a box-office turkey, pulling in only $26,525,000, which wasn't all that impressive for a film that featured a big star like Beatty and had grabbed several national magazine covers in its publicity push. *Bulworth*'s budget was $30 million, so it failed to even make up its costs.

Big-screen superstardom was still eluding Halle. She would turn back to the small screen next.

"If I were white, I would capture the world."

—DOROTHY DANDRIDGE

"Dorothy was trying to carve a niche for
a black leading lady back in 1953,
and I'm still trying to carve that same
niche in 1999. We share that struggle."

—HALLE BERRY

SEVEN

Big on the Small Screen

One was not yet twenty when they met. The other had been dead for almost twenty years. They could have been sisters—the same sweet glowing skin (like honey poured in sunlight), the same soft curly hair (short and dark as a summer night), the same small sexy smile (as white as clouds and somehow as far away). They were both born in the same hospital, decades apart. They had never met in life, and here they were, meeting across that thing that comes after. The one had never seen a black woman like the other before. She was a star, a black star, passionate, sophisticated, full of power. The one had seen blacks in movies before— Song of the South, *shuffling slaves, switchblade wielders in blaxploitation flicks—but nothing like this, nothing like what she was witnessing in this movie,* Carmen Jones. *The colors, the emotion, the motion—it captivated her, fascinated her, held her in its grip. The other stared back through the television screen, through the years, through the acres of broken hearts and broken bottles, through the medicine cabi-*

net stocked with Dexamyl and Dexedrine and ben-
zedrine and Tofranil and thyroid pills and antidepres-
sants, through the rooms of nervous black girls await-
ing their turns at auditions, through the soft fabric of
a blue scarf tied around her head as she lay naked on a
bathroom floor . . .

Kevin Hooks was surprised to see Halle Berry when he ran into her in the Pasadena Civic Auditorium on August 26, 2000. He was attending an Emmy cere-mony—not the one the public is used to seeing on tele-vision, where various small screen stars from the net-works and the cable stations gather to fete themselves, award prizes to themselves, and celebrate their own industry because not many other people will. This Emmy ceremony was for the "creative arts"—the behind the scenes players, the producers and technical workers, the people who aren't stars but who work hard to make the stars who they are. Hooks had won an Emmy in the category of outstanding children's program for produc-ing a movie for the Disney Channel called *The Color of Friendship;* Berry was there to support some friends and colleagues—makeup artists and the like—who had worked on her HBO biopic *Introducing Dorothy Dandridge.* Halle couldn't stop talking about Kevin's award, and how happy she was that he had won it. Wasn't it all too crazy? They had both gone from work-ing on the low-budget film *Strictly Business* to where they were now, him with an award and Halle up for an award at the main ceremony in two weeks. She asked

Hooks if she could hold his prize—just to gauge its weight, just to feel it in her hand. He told her she would get her own awards soon enough.

Halle Berry had been obsessed with Dorothy Dandridge ever since she was eighteen years old and saw her on television for the first time. She had never seen a star like Dandridge before. She didn't know black women came in this particular variety: the glamorous star variety, the Ava, Marilyn, and Grace variety. Later, when she signed with Vincent Cirrincione, the idea of turning Dandridge's life into a film surfaced again in Halle's mind. Halle's manager told her to "find a project you really want to do" and pursue it. Halle told the *Cleveland Plain Dealer:* "The most identifiable similarity is that we're both two black women trying to make it in an industry that doesn't make much of a place for people like us. Dorothy was trying to carve a niche for a black leading lady back in 1953, and I'm still trying to carve that same niche in 1999. We share that struggle."

Halle and Dorothy had other things in common. It was almost as if the two actresses, in certain ways, were, in their lives, playing versions of each other—an acting duet played out across the decades. Both Halle and Dorothy were born in the same hospital in Cleveland—City Hospital. Halle told the *Cleveland Plain Dealer* in 1999: "I felt that connection with her. Since she was from Cleveland, I felt like I should be the one to play her, I'm from Cleveland, too. Obviously, you don't have to be from Cleveland to play Dorothy Dandridge, but that certainly gave me the license to say I should be the one to play her."

Dorothy Jean Dandridge was born on November 9, 1922. Like Halle, her parents had marital problems; Dorothy's mother, Ruby, walked out on Dorothy's father, Cyrus, five months before Dorothy's birth (Ruby was a lesbian and left to be with another woman). Dorothy's psychic trauma has eerie echo's of Halle's own emotional struggle. Donald Bogle, in his book *Dorothy Dandridge: A Biography*, writes that "the little girl who would grow up to be one of her era's most beautiful women and its most famous African American actress— came into the world at the heart of a heated domestic discord that, in its own quiet, unstated way, would trouble and haunt her. . . . Throughout her life, she would struggle to understand her parents but mainly to piece together the puzzle of her own identity; to discover and define herself first as a daughter, then as a sister, a wife, a mother . . . and actress, and finally as the most unexpected and elusive of personages, a black film star in a Hollywood that worshiped her, yet at the same time, clearly made no place for her." The same passage could have been written about Halle.

Dandridge was a screen actress, a nightclub singer, and a media personality. She starred in more than twenty films in America and Europe at a time when being a black star was basically an oxymoron. She refused to play maids and slaves and her roles broke through stereotype. She appeared in MGM's *The Bright Road* (1953) opposite Harry Belafonte (Dandridge played a schoolteacher, Belafonte played a principal with a crush on her). It was one of the first studio films to present blacks not as problems or issues but as human beings, dealing with human issues of love and longing. Dandridge also starred in the Samuel Goldwyn production of *Porgy and Bess* (1959), a feature film version of the George Gershwin musical drama.

Like Halle, Dorothy had her insecurities and anxieties. Like Halle, she often linked herself with men who would prove to be unhealthy for her, or who would go on to mistreat or abuse her. Sidney Poitier, who co-starred in *Porgy and Bess* alongside Dandridge, once wrote of the awful manner in which Otto Preminger, Dandridge's lover/director, treated her on set. "It happened, I think, on the first day I started to work," Poitier wrote. "Otto Preminger jumped on Dorothy Dandridge in a shocking and totally unexpected way. She had done something that wasn't quite the way he wanted it. . . . Dorothy Dandridge, visibly shaken, started the scene again, hoping to recapture the missing ingredient and save herself from further embarrassment. She hadn't proceeded very far before he exploded again. . . . And on he went. . . . Dandridge fell apart. . . . On that day I learned the serene look [she] wore only served to mask the fears, frustration, and insecurities that were tumbling around inside her all the time."

And, like Halle, Dorothy had her share of triumphs. Dandridge was the first African-American woman to be nominated for a best actress award, for her 1954 performance as the title character in *Carmen Jones.*

Watching Dandridge's performance today, it still holds up. There are other major talents in the film—Belafonte and Pearl Bailey among them—but Dandridge commands the screen from the moment she enters a soldiers' mess hall in a fire-red skirt and an insolent smirk.

Carmen Jones is an all-black musical version of Bizet's opera *Carmen* with words by Oscar Hammerstein II, and direction by Otto Preminger. It's too bad that the studio didn't allow Belafonte and Dandridge to sing their own parts (they both have fine voices), but, then again, Audrey Hepburn didn't get to sing her own part in *My Fair Lady* and her performance still came through. (It should be noted that Dandridge was an accomplished vocalist and Hepburn was only an average one; the DVD version of *My Fair Lady* features a few alternate musical sequences with Hepburn's own vocals. They prove that the movie was clearly better served by having someone else sing Hepburn's part.) In any case, in *Carmen Jones,* Dandridge, even without singing a lick, hits all the right notes. She fistfights and she seduces, she smiles and she snarls, she seems equally comfortably biting Belafonte in the arm in a dusty struggle as she is making love to him in another scene. Dandridge isn't interested in playing sweet, and that's what fills her performance with such flavor. There is an unexpected tanginess to her acting that is almost unprecedented in cinema; in the decades since, others have sought to imitate it, but it has never been duplicated.

• • •

Halle's manager made a call to Earl Mills, Dandridge's manager and the author of a book about her life, and learned that his work had already been optioned. In fact, around the time that Halle began to pursue turning Dandridge's life story into a movie, several other black actresses including Janet Jackson and Whitney Houston began to look into such a project as well. In a way it was a bit sad. The fact that so many African-American actresses were interested in telling this tale was an indication of how few tales African-American actresses had gotten to tell. Years after her death, Dandridge still stood out—no other black actress had yet risen to her level of stardom and accomplishment. No black actress had completed her journey and won an Academy Award for leading actress. A few had been nominated—Diana Ross, Angela Bassett—but the goal had not been reached. Halle told the *New York Times* in 2002: "I got discouraged when I heard they were both trying to make it because I figured they had a lot more money and power. So I thought I would bow out gracefully. And it was Vince who said, 'Why bow out gracefully? You've been working on this for seven years.'" Halle's manager kept checking in with Mills, and when the option ran out, Halle and her production team stepped in.

Halle tried in vain to get a film studio to finance the production of a Dandridge biopic as a feature film. She believed that it only made sense that a bio about a *film* actress should be a *film*. But in the end she went with HBO. "It's not just acceptable to jump into film and television, it's desirable," Halle told the *Cleveland Plain*

Dealer. "It keeps you from getting trapped into one type of role. A true leading lady role like Dorothy Dandridge is not going to happen in features. You make it happen on television."

Halle not only took on the lead role, she also signed on as executive producer. Halle told *Movieline* in 2001: "HBO allowed me to be a real producer. Even when it got into financial trouble, I gave up some of my salary; I helped make decisions on where to spend money. I knew we had to put as much money onto the screen so actors had to be paid less, because period pieces are really hard to do. . . . There are [favorite old films I'd like to remake], but honestly, I'm not going to say them, because I did that with *Dorothy Dandridge* and then everybody wanted to do it!"

In June 2002, I chatted with Martha Coolidge, the director of *Introducing Dorothy Dandridge,* about how she first hooked up with Halle and the HBO movie. Coolidge told me: "It's an incredible story and I really wanted to do the project. I had never met Halle when I went into the first meeting. I had seen her in several movies, but hadn't met her before. She was really beautiful but really feisty in the meeting with the HBO executives. She was going on about when she wanted the picture to be released, and just sort of producer things. About not getting lumped into Black History Month and why is that the only month they get. I was really impressed with her fire and just said to myself, she's really got the passion and she's gonna be great in the part. I was really excited to work with her. She's a terrific professional, just a wonderful person and a great role model."

The project was Halle's, but she didn't feel like Dandridge until two days before the shooting. Dandridge's manager, during the making of the film, brought by thirteen big boxes of mementos of his life with the fallen star. The boxes contained scraps of paper, telegrams, letters, photos, pill bottles, clothes. He refused to just leave them, and he checked into a hotel to be close to all the knickknacks. One item was particularly special: a creamy blue evening gown Dandridge had once worn.

Mills gave the blue dress to Halle. Usually Halle found that she was a tough fit; she had to take dresses she wore in at the waist. This dress fit her perfectly. She broke down and cried. The dress fit. Halle says she isn't religious, she doesn't know what to call whatever the power sitting up in the sky is—Buddha, Jesus, Allah—but she says she is spiritual. And when she tried on Dorothy's dress, and it slipped on her like it had been tailored for her, she felt the hand of fate touch her on the shoulder. This was her dress. This was her picture. This was her time. Halle kept the dress on a mannequin in her family room during the entire *Dorothy Dandridge* shoot.

The contours of *Introducing Dorothy Dandridge* are simple and classic. In tried-and-true biopic form, Dandridge's story is told in an extended flashback; as the actress talks on the phone and assembles a photo collage, she thinks back on the significant moments of her life. Most biopics tend to bite off more than they can chew.

Most people, even celebrities, tend not to have lives that fit comfortably into dramatic story arcs. It's often better, for the purposes of drama, to select a particularly meaningful and representative moment in a subject's life and extend and dramatize that, rather than examining a subject's life from birth to death. *Introducing* tries to tell the whole story when perhaps an introduction would have sufficed.

Still, the breadth of the movie allows Halle to give the most complete performance of her career. She plays Dandridge with a mix of brashness and tenderness, sadness and anger, sexiness and early innocence. She ages her character well too, from a strutting hot young thing to a worldly, boozy middle-aged woman. The script is somewhat stiff and without poetry, and some of the lines of dialogue are somewhat flat—someone actually has to deliver the line "Whoever sang that song . . . I'm gonna make them a star." Harrison Ford once said famously to George Lucas about his wooden dialogue in the Star Wars movies "George, you can type this shit but you sure can't say it." That sentiment certainly applies to some of *Introducing Dorothy Dandridge*.

And yet time after time in this movie, Halle's line readings are a wonder. The way she tells off Darryl Zanuck when he appears to be trying to pick her up. Her sharp, no-nonsense admonition to her manager for him to give her all the bad news straight up, with no sugar. Halle's performance also goes deeper than the words: the looks she gives—blends of hurt and defiance—when, time and time again, she is not allowed, because she is black, to use the rest rooms at clubs in which she is performing. And Halle does a great job lip-syncing to Dorothy Dandridge's music; she gives a visual performance that sometimes outdoes the vocals—dancing, smiling, kicking her shoes off.

Coolidge told me: "I think one of the more difficult scenes to play was the molestation rape by the mother's lover. That was a tricky scene to lay, let me tell you. She was just incredible. Her ability to make things real for herself and express that. The scene of the first night with her first husband. Finding out her child was retarded. But almost as amazing was her ability to lip-sync and dance. This is not a woman who was trained as a singer and dancer. We started her dancing, started rehearsing seven weeks prior to production. She first learned to tap, and then we'd add a dance every week. First tap, then once she got a hold on tap, she'd move to a different thing. Meanwhile she took voice lessons to learn how to breathe and sing—she had to learn how to sing to be believable doing it."

The film is also beautifully produced. Made inexpensively—thanks to Halle's canny producing—it manages to somehow look lavish and detailed. Halle fought for every penny of the budget, and was willing to go to great lengths to make sure the quality of the project was never compromised. Coolidge said to me in an interview: "It's funny thinking about all this. . . . I was remembering in *Dorothy* we had to do some severe budget cutting just to get the whole movie into the package, to fit it into the budget. It was below $10 million. They wanted it significantly below $10 million. There was a lot of negotiating. But the original budget, when they actually budgeted the script they had, it was well over $10 million, so we knew there was some cutting that had to be done. In the end we had to slash the exterior Academy Awards, the 1955 awards. That had to be taken out, even though I knew, Halle and myself and everyone loved that scene, it was not a plot-oriented scene. It didn't necessarily further the movie, and Halle just missed it terribly as did we all. And finally when push came to shove, she said, 'You know, Martha, even though we have an interior Academy Awards scene, for Dorothy Dandridge to have walked down that red carpet was significant. Dorothy has to walk down that red carpet—that's what's important about that scene. She was the first African-American woman to ever walk down that red carpet as a lead actress nominee and we've got to have it in the movie.' And so she paid for the day out of her own salary. And she was so right. When we finished the movie and we were saying things to each other, sending little notes, I told her not only did she give Dorothy Dandridge back to the world, she was also giving her people another role model in herself, in Halle Berry."

In the end, *Introducing Dorothy Dandridge* becomes that rare biopic in which the talent of the actor is shown to match, or even exceed, the talent of the person portrayed. When performers play performers they put themselves on public trial. In every scene, with every camera angle, with every utterance, we judge them: Are they as beautiful as the star they are imitating? Do they have comparable magnetism? Do they measure up? Sometimes a star can get by with an easy judgment. Dennis Quaid's portrayal of Jerry Lee Lewis in *Great Balls of Fire!* (1989) was not as electrifying or as edgy as the original, but because not many young moviegoers have a clear impression of Lewis, Quaid's broadly drawn version sufficed. In the TV movie *Norma Jean & Marilyn* (1996), two sexy young actresses, Mira Sorvino and Ashley Judd, attempt to portray the fallen screen icon at different stages of her life, but despite their individual charms, neither really measures up to the original. Robert Downey Jr.'s haunted turn as Charlie Chaplin in *Chaplin* (1992) captured much of the silent filmmaker's comic genius (though the direction and screenplay were wanting). And Jennifer Lopez's role as the *tejano* singer Selena in the 1997 movie of the same name was a rare example of a movie in which an actress displayed as much charisma as her subject (and, in subsequent years, Lopez has built up an even bigger legend).

Introducing Dorothy Dandridge was a case where the death of one star helped give birth to another. Playing a screen legend is a bid at immortality; however, it is usually a losing one that makes the living actor seem small by comparison. Halle, by showing as much sexual charisma, charm, and acting ability as Dandridge, posed this silent question: Isn't she just as big a star? Ironically, Dorothy Dandridge provided Halle Berry a better part than Halle had ever gotten in her life or Dandridge had ever gotten before her death.

Dandridge's life story is a tragedy. In her autobiography *Everything and Nothing: The Dorothy Dandridge Tragedy*, written with Earl Conrad, she writes: "My gross earnings had exceeded a million dollars when I was in my mid-thirties, and I was the only Negro actress to achieve both film stardom and a nomination for a best actress Academy Award. . . . First I learned that I was broke from poor investments in Arizona oil wells. . . . A day or two later I was in court to divorce my second husband, a handsome white man, Jack Denison, with whom several years of living had become a nightmare. A few days after that I was legally evicted from my sixty-five-thousand-dollar showplace home in the hills overlooking Hollywood. As if this were not enough, just as I was losing my fortune, my husband, and my home, my retarded nineteen-year-old daughter Lynn was returned to me. All of these events converged with paralyzing swiftness, with crisis upon crisis. At the end, all I wanted was to take a long walk off Malibu Beach. My career seemed crushed and over with."

Dandridge's life was a tragedy, but Halle felt her movie could give people hope—after all, there were happy moments in Dorothy's life, and moments of triumph as well. And the fact that the movie even got made was, in and of itself, a happy ending to Dandridge's tale. Halle said: "I'm one to tell you how much things have changed for the better since Dorothy's day. I just spent four months playing a woman who couldn't walk into the front entrance of clubs where she was playing. She couldn't even dip her toe in a hotel pool. And she certainly wouldn't have been able to produce a movie about the life of anybody she admired. I'm able to do that."

Coolidge told me: "I think the scene that moved us all was the swimming pool, where she puts a toe in a swimming pool and she comes by later and they're scrubbing out the pool. That was the scene everybody in the crew was just stunned by and moved by. The other one is Earl Mills handing her the cup and saying pee in the cup [because the club wouldn't let Dandridge use white rest rooms]. They brought home the reality of how recent this kind of discrimination was—and is."

Halle also found some personal catharsis in telling Dandridge's story. She saw the way one Hollywood story ended, and she didn't want her own story to end that way. Halle told the *Cleveland Plain Dealer* in 1999: "Well, like Dorothy Dandridge I had this real need to be accepted and loved by people. For Dorothy, this incredible vulnerability was the result of a tumultuous childhood, of always being judged superficially, of the criticism and the racism. She needed to be loved because she didn't love herself enough. All of that fed her vulnerability, and I can relate to at least part of that. The need for love and acceptance drove me back into performing, too. But I'm no longer that person. I used to want everyone to love me. I now know that when you love yourself enough, you stop begging everyone else to love you."

Kevin Hooks, Halle's old director, was right. In the end, Halle hauled in the hardware for her turn in *Introducing*

Dorothy Dandridge. First, the TV movie won a Golden Globe for best performance by an actress in a miniseries. An exultant Halle, whose mother had told her to enjoy the moment, took the stage. "Well, Mom . . . I'm enjoying it!" she said. She then addressed Eric directly. "You have given me the biggest gift anybody can give me and that is the freedom to be who I am and for loving me anyway." Finally, she spoke of Dorothy Dandridge: "Tonight, as you honor me, whom you really honor is the eminent Dorothy Dandridge. She never got to stand here and be recognized by her peers, but because she lived, I am able to. Thank you so much."

Introducing kept cleaning up. It went on to win an NAACP Image Award for outstanding actress in a television movie/miniseries dramatic special, a Screen Actors Guild award for outstanding performance by a female actor in a television movie or miniseries, and, in its perhaps biggest victory, it won five Emmys, including one for outstanding lead actress in a miniseries or a movie. In her acceptance speech at the Emmys, Halle said: "Wherever Dorothy Dandridge is right now, she is standing tall and proud. Thank you to my community, who picks me up when I'm down and never, ever lets go."

Halle treasured every award. She told *Movieline* in 2001: "It meant a lot. It instantly gave me credibility; not only with my peers but within the industry."

At an intersection in Los Angeles, however, that hard-won credibility was about to be stripped away.

"I watched your six o'clock news today. It's straight *tabloid!* You had a minute and a half of that lady riding a bike naked in Central Park; on the other hand, you had less than a minute of hard national and international news! It was all sex, scandal, brutal crime, sports, children with incurable diseases, and lost puppies. So, I don't think I'll listen to any protestations of high standards of journalism when you're right down on the streets soliciting audiences like the rest of us! Look, all I'm saying is if you're going to hustle, at least do it right!"

—FAYE DUNAWAY, *Network* (1976)

"I learned this wasn't about a car accident. It was about facing fear."

—HALLE BERRY

EIGHT

The Accident

There is, for her, only before and after. She says she doesn't remember the middle of it. She says that there at the center, where so much happened, there is only an absence of experience, a long nothing, a blank sheet that she doesn't recall ever erasing. That's what she says. She says she remembers hanging out with a girlfriend, catching up, snacking, talking late into the night, like girlfriends do. Then she drove home. Then something happened that she doesn't remember, that she says she can't remember. After that thing, whatever it was, she was back at her house, blood gushing from her forehead. Then there was the press, the rumors, the lawyers. But as to what it was about, she says she doesn't remember any of it. All there is is this jump, from here to there, from the road to her house, from hanging out to controversy. Here's what she says she doesn't remember: the sickening crunch of metal against metal; something cutting into her forehead, almost to the bone; a Pontiac Sunfire, crushed and burning, sending smoke up into the night sky. All of

that happened—there were witnesses and press reports.
But she doesn't remember any of it. That's what she
says.

This time Halle was the one leaving. Her whole life had
been a series of accidents, some happy, some sad, and
throughout her life there had been a series of men, all
walking away. Looking back at her life, they seemed to
be walking forward. Their faces, and their footsteps,
haunted her. Her father, who left her family. The mystery man who knocked the hearing out of her ear. Her
ex-husband, David Justice. Now, at an intersection of
West Hollywood at around 2:30 A.M. on February 23, it
was her time to leave.

Halle had been hanging out that night with a girlfriend—nothing special, just her and a friend, eating
chips, drinking Diet Coke, the usual. Halle then drove
herself home sometime after in a rented white Chevy
Blazer. It was past 2:00 A.M. and she was passing
through West Hollywood. Then it happened. According
to numerous reports, Halle went through a red light and
slammed into a 1996 Pontiac Sunfire that was being
driven by Heta Raythatha, a Santa Monica real estate
agent and part-time accountant. The crash opened up a
gash on Halle's forehead; it also broke Raythatha's wrist.
Halle, without stopping to check on the other driver or
exchange information, drove home. Marisa Meola, who
was driving about fifteen feet behind Raythatha's car
when it was hit by Berry's SUV, told *People* in 2000: "It
was a brutal, brutal car accident—that girl could have

been dead. To drive away with blatant disregard? I'm extremely outraged."

After Meola called an ambulance, Raythatha was taken to Ceders-Sinai Medical Center. Raythatha still didn't quite know what had hit her and she certainly didn't know *who* had hit her. In the hospital, she happened to spy Halle, dressed in jeans and a tank top and sporting a bandage on her head. Raythatha, in the midst of her pain, took the time to note that she had just seen a genuine movie star: Halle Berry. A few days later, starstruck admiration would give way to outrage when Raythatha found out that Halle was the driver of the car that struck her. Raythatha told *InStyle* in 2000: "[Berry] left me in a smoking car wreck. She sped off and made no attempt to get me help. I find everything she has told the press regarding her alleged blackout completely unbelievable. The fact that the DA let her off easy and she is trying to portray herself as a victim is very saddening."

On March 31, 2000, Halle was indicted on charges of leaving the scene of an accident, a misdemeanor. The charge, however, came with serious penalties: a year in county jail and a $10,000 fine. Blair Berk, Halle Berry's attorney, issued a statement on her behalf after the district attorney announced his decision to charge her with a misdemeanor in connection with the car accident. Berk announced: "Halle is obviously pleased by the DA's determination that felony charges should be rejected and are not justified in connection with this unfortunate traffic accident. The past several weeks have been very difficult for her. There has been an enormous amount of misinformation circulated about Halle and this accident, and Halle is anxious to set the record straight. The appropriate place to do this, however, given the pending legal matter, is in a court of law."

Halle's lawyer went on: "There are a few things I can say at this time. As you all know, Halle suffered a severe blow to the head in the accident. It left a gash in her forehead that required more than twenty stitches to close. The idea that Halle intended to flee the scene of an accident is simply not true. We are confident that once all the true facts come to light, this will be clear. It is undisputed that Halle received medical treatment at the hospital after the accident; she voluntarily reported the accident to a police officer at that time, and again reported the accident to the police the next day. There is another point I'd like to make. Despite some scurrilous insinuations, Halle was never at any time 'driving under the influence.' As a Sheriff's Department spokesman confirmed early on, neither drugs nor alcohol played any part in this accident. This was also confirmed by personnel at the hospital where Halle was treated after the accident. The fact is, Halle did not drink any alcohol that day or night, and she most definitely doesn't take drugs.

"There have also been a series of false and misleading reports that Halle was somehow involved in a hit-and-run accident in the past. This is simply not true. Halle has had only one other minor traffic accident in her entire life. The police did conduct a traffic investigation following that accident in 1995, but they quickly concluded there was no evidence of any wrongdoing whatsoever on Halle's part. As to any other rumors that have been reported, the DA's own independent investigation has confirmed that those rumors are a total fiction. In any case, now that the DA has made his decision and rejected felony charges, I am confident that the true facts will come out in court, and we are looking forward to resolving this entire matter as soon as possible."

For Halle, the next few days were a torture. She avoided the press. She avoided public outings. She found that she couldn't eat, she couldn't sleep. She was waiting for the situation to be resolved legally so she could finally tell her side of the story. According to Halle, when she got home, Benet was there and he took her back to the accident scene but nobody was there; they then went on to Cedars-Sinai Hospital. According to hospital records, by that point, an hour and forty minutes had passed since the accident.

Finally, on May 10, 2000, in Beverly Hills Superior Court, Halle pleaded no contest to the charge and received three years probation, two hundred hours of community service, and a $13,500 fine. The no-contest plea was a bit of legal strategy—it accepted the penalties but left open the possibility that Halle could deny the allegations in other proceedings. Halle had her say in court, making this statement: "Your Honor, I would like the court to know that I have taken this matter very seriously from the very beginning. I am pleased that this can be resolved. And I'm very relieved that the true facts of this case have finally come out."

Next, Halle set out to win the case in the court of public opinion. One of her first stops was NBC's *Today* show, where host Matt Lauer grilled her over her plea and her actions.

LAUER: Why plead no contest? Why not go through and say, "I'm not . . . I'm not guilty"?

MS. BERRY: Well, because pleading no contest isn't admitting any guilt. That's something that I think a lot of people don't understand. The judge himself yesterday in open court allowed me to maintain my innocence. Pleading no contest for me was a way for me to take responsibility for my physical action.

LAUER: Saying, "Yes, I did leave the scene of this traffic accident"?

MS. BERRY: I did leave. Yes. But I feel like I have a very defensible reason for leaving, because of my head injury, which put me in a state of mind that did not make me responsible in that moment. And the judge in open court admitted that yesterday.

LAUER: The plea does carry the same weight as conviction by California law.

MS. BERRY: Yes.

LAUER: So in the eyes of the court, you have been convicted of this crime. But you think that the technicality . . . it's really semantics here.

MS. BERRY: It's semantics, exactly.

Halle also defended herself to Diane Sawyer on ABC.

SAWYER: Well, here's what the judge said, three years probation, two hundred hours of community service, and $13,500 in fines and penalties. That is the punishment that the judge handed out yesterday to actress Halle Berry, who did no contest to leaving the scene of a traffic accident. There have been so many rumors surrounding this event. Was she on drugs? Was she speeding? Why did it take an hour and forty minutes to report what happened? Well, this morning we're going to hear more from Halle Berry as she tells us what she says happened that night. All right, let me go back. You leave your girlfriend's house, you say, not a drop of alcohol.

MS. BERRY: Not a drop.

SAWYER: No drugs of any kind?

MS. BERRY: I don't do drugs. No drugs of any kind.

SAWYER: Were you speeding?

MS. BERRY: No. I was not speeding. And the investigative reports from the police department have confirmed that. I was not speeding. I was wearing my seat belt. I approached the intersection two blocks from my house at Sunset and Doheny, and the last thing I remember about approaching that intersection was something dark coming from my right. The next thing I remember after that is

being at my house, blood pouring from my forehead. . . .

SAWYER: So you don't have a memory of a green
light, yellow light, any light?

MS. BERRY: No. I just remember approaching that
intersection and then being at my house. Now
you're looking at me like how could that be.

SAWYER: How could that be?

MS. BERRY: And you know what, Diane, these were
my very same concerns. Imagine being at your
house bleeding, car crashed, not knowing how or
why or what happened to you, or God forbid,
something else.

On May 7, 2001, it was announced that Raythatha's
civil suit against Halle had been settled for an undis-
closed sum. Halle told *Movieline* in 2001, when asked
whose fault the accident was: "It was undetermined. I
was never cited or charged for it because the witnesses
said conflicting things. The side of my car and the front
of hers were damaged." She also said: "My medical con-
dition forced me to react the way I did." Raythatha's
camp seems to have given up on any back-and-forth
charges of blame. When I asked Raythatha's lawyer,
Gloria Allred, for a comment on the case in June 2002,
she told me "The matter is resolved."

Halle also took her case to the black press. She knew

she was an icon to many African-American girls, an inspiration, a success story. She didn't want her star tainted. So she spilled her guts. Halle told *Jet* on September 11, 2000: "It was important for me as the woman I say I am to take some responsibility. To be guilty I had to have knowingly and willfully left that scene, and I did not do that. I did the best I could given what happened to me, and I was woman enough to take responsibility for my physical actions even though I did not intentionally do it."

Halle must have been shaken by the fact that, under duress, she had walked away. But there was one major difference between Halle's actions and those of the men who had walked away from her in her past. At the time of the accident, according to Halle, she was bleeding and confused. Now that she had her senses back, she tried to do what her father never attempted to do. She walked back to face her troubles and take some responsibility. Halle told *Ebony* in 2000: "I learned this wasn't about a car accident. It was about facing fear. My whole life I've had the fear that I was going to be abandoned. It goes back to my childhood and not having my father. I dealt with it in my divorce [from David Justice]. And, when this unfortunate thing happened, I had to face that fear again. . . . I thought the public would abandon me. That I'd lose everything I've worked so hard for. That I would be tainted goods."

For Halle, the accident was also a turning point in her relations with men. Before the accident, she could never quite trust them, it seems. After all, it's easy to be with a movie star when times are good, when the hits are coming, when the cameras are flashing and the jobs and invitations and awards are rolling in. Somewhere, in the back of her mind, in one of the valves of her heart, was always the suspicion that love, at least the variety she tended to get, could not survive the bad times. After all, she had seen it with her father; she had also seen it in her own life. But Benet, in this instance, was different. And that was unexpected. As Halle told *Ebony:* "As the weeks went by, I thought, 'Wow, he's still here.' And not just loving me. Loving me hard. He showed me when I was too weak to stand, he would hold me up. When I was too fragile to think, he'd help me figure it out. When I was too scared to face another day, he'd be my rock."

Around the time of her accident troubles, Halle scored one of her biggest hits. *X-Men* (2000) is a highly entertaining comic book movie. It has fine actors: Patrick Stewart, Hugh Jackman, and, of course, Halle; it has a top-notch director, Bryan Singer, who helmed the critically acclaimed 1995 mystery *The Usual Suspects;* and it has an intriguing plot that doesn't skimp on the action for the kiddies, but it also has deeper themes that adults can respect. Halle first met with Singer to talk about *X-Men* because she was a big admirer of *The Usual Suspects.* During the meeting, when he discussed his intention to bring in award-winning actors such as Ian McKellen (who would play Magneto) and Anna Paquin (who would play Rogue), Halle became excited about taking part—she wanted to work with top talent, and the names

Singer was throwing out signaled to her that *X-Men* wouldn't be some crummy comic book flick, but a real film, with real heart. Since she was coming off of *Dorothy Dandridge,* she was ready to slip into an ensemble, one in which she wouldn't have the burden of having to carry the whole movie.

X-Men, which was adapted from the popular Marvel comic book of the same name, is based on the conceit that humans are evolving, but only some of them. While a handful are developing weird, superherolike powers, many of the rest are scared—and are prepared to discriminate against, even eliminate, the new breed of *X-Men.* Stewart plays Professor X, a visionary mutant who has set up a school for X-Men (in, of all places, Westchester) to help them integrate into society. Halle Berry plays Storm, a teacher at the school, a mutant with a shock of shoulder-length off-white hair who has the power to control the weather. Stewart, Storm, and the other X-Men (including Wolverine, played by Jackman) uncover a plot by an evil mutant named Magneto (a supremely modulated McKellen) to turn the world into mutants (and, in the process, eventually kill them).

Halle told *Ebony* in August 2000: "The mutants face many of the same obstacles that we do as African Americans. They're struggling to find equality within a society of nonmutants who fear them out of ignorance. Storm reminds everyone that, if anything is to change, we have to educate people out of their ignorance. That's the substance of who Storm is to me."

In *X-Men,* Halle looks great (her costume is black leather with a black cape) and never acts down to the material. She does battle with half-men/half-toads and does so with style and a bit of understated humor. She even delivers the line "You know what happens to a toad when it's struck by lightning? Same thing that happens to everything else" with something resembling sincerity. After all the low-budget movies Halle had suffered through over the course of her career, it's uplifting to see her, in one scene, fly up an elevator shaft, buoyed by winds, surrounded by bolts of electricity, dressed in a cool form-fitting leather costume, supported by high-quality special effects, and, at long last, a major production budget. *X-Men,* which had a $75 million budget, took in $157,299,000 in the United States, making it Halle's highest-grossing film; she also signed on to do the sequel.

Swordfish was another major Hollywood-style film for Halle; she got to dress up, act tough, and star alongside John Travolta. The film is about a reactionary militant genius (Travolta) and his assistant (Halle) who hire a superhacker (Hugh Jackman again) to commit a large-scale cybertheft. Halle—as in *The Flintstones* and *Bulworth*—once again plays a character who betrays others and isn't quite who she seems to be. There's a particularly strong scene in which Jackman, while Travolta and Halle look on amused, is forced to hack into the Department of Defense computers within sixty seconds while he is, shall we say, being distracted orally by a blonde and menaced by a gun. Halle impressed her fellow actors on the film by her refusal to accept being treated with kid gloves. In one scene in the movie, Jackman throws Halle out of a trailer, but in the initial take he did it gently. Halle said to him: "No, throw me out of the f'ing trailer—this isn't believable!" Jackman, a down-to-earth Aussie, respected her commitment to her craft—and so, in the next take, threw her on her behind. *Swordfish* sometimes strays a little over the top, and its theme has no larger resonance, but it's still an entertaining and effective thriller, due in no small measure to Halle, who smolders in every scene she's in. *Swordfish,* however, wasn't a hit. It only made $69,772,000 at the box office—disappointing, especially for a Travolta film, and even more disappointing for a movie whose budget was $80 million.

But the film became somewhat notorious, despite its light take at the box office. *Swordfish* represented the first film in which Halle had displayed any nudity— a completely and shamelessly gratuitous scene in which Halle is sunbathing topless for no real reason. It advances the plot not a whit, and it deepens her character not one iota; it's a sequence that seems purely designed for fourteen-year-old boys—and every other man on the planet. Halle told the *New York Times* in 2002: "I told Joel that I didn't want to go topless, and he listened to my reasons and told me to go ahead anyway, and I did," she says. Rumors began to fly that the studio had had to pay, and pay big, to get her to drop her top. One figure that was batted around: Halle was paid $500,000 for the nude scene. She denied any specific payment for the scene and joked that her breasts were worth much more than $250,000 each. She was actually paid $2.5 million for her role in the movie—for the entire part.

For Halle, showing her breasts was, in part, part of the process of breaking away from Justice. In her mind, he was the type of man who would have said "Not my wife" had she told him she was filming a scene revealing her body. Her new husband was, like her, an artist. He understood the concept of creative freedom, the need for self-expression. According to Halle, Benet helped talk her into the nude scene in *Swordfish*. Benet told her that she was uninhibited at home—buying art that celebrated the unclothed form, having conversations with him while she was seated on the toilet. Now he wanted her to finally show her sexy side, her erotic side, the part of her self she had always hidden from the camera and the public and the world. In other countries, in places in Europe and Africa, women strolled beaches naked and walked through villages with their breasts bared; why, then, should Halle buy into the irrational American fear of the naked, natural human figure? In the past, she had played crackheads and teachers, hookers and homegirls and stewardesses. Now it was time to reveal herself as a sexual being—it would be part of unveiling herself as a serious actress.

Nudity is one of the quickest ways to get on top in Hollywood, and one of the fastest ways to be relegated to the bottom. Take a look at all those soft-porn films that air late at night on Cinemax and Showtime and

HBO—there's very little crossover between the ingenues rolling around in threesomes and the women you see cast in mainstream Hollywood fare. But, then again, Hollywood actresses discover, time and time again, that when an actress drops her bra or her panties, the sound echoes around Tinseltown. Sharon Stone had been knocking around Hollywood for years in B-minus films like *King Solomon's Mines* (1985), *Allan Quartermain and the Lost City of Gold* (1987), and *Police Academy 4: Citizens on Patrol* (1987). But after she posed for *Playboy* in 1990 and flashed her nether regions in *Basic Instinct* (1992), suddenly she was Hollywood's most prized female thespian.

Hollywood also rewards women who play sexually available characters, whether they're nude in the project or not. Jodie Foster *(Taxi Driver)*, Brooke Shields *(Pretty Baby)*, Susan Sarandon *(Pretty Baby)*, and Julia Roberts *(Pretty Woman)* all established their careers by playing prostitutes; Elisabeth Shue *(Leaving Las Vegas)* and Stone *(Casino)* got their only Oscar nominations for hooker roles; Jane Fonda *(Klute)*, Kim Basinger *(L.A. Confidential)*, Mira Sorvino *(Mighty Aphrodite)* all won their first Oscars for hooker roles. Hollywood just loves it when women strip down and/or play dirty—especially if they're really smart (both Shue and Sorvino were former Harvard students). It's telling to observe that this has been going on for some time in the performing arts. As Addison Dewitt, the character played by George Sanders in *All About Eve* (1950) notes about Margo Channing, the character played by Bette Davis: "Margo

Channing is a star of the theater. She made her stage debut at the age of four in *Midsummer Night's Dream*, playing a fairy. She entered, quite unexpectedly, stark naked. She has been a star ever since."

Halle has had an evolving attitude toward nudity over the years. In one of her early movies, *The Last Boy Scout* (1991), in which she played a stripper, she was shocked to find, after she had verbally agreed to do the picture, that her contract had a clause requiring nudity. She was already in rehearsals when the contract was presented to her to sign. She badly needed the money and the part, but she nonetheless refused to do the scene and declined to sign the contract; in the end, a body double was hired and filming went ahead. In 1995, Halle told *Newsday* that she didn't want to show her "goodies" in public. She asserted, jokingly, "No frontal nudity. Only backal nudity. I'll show my butt." She went on to say, "At this time in my life—and I'll never say never—I'm just not comfortable with frontal nudity. . . . They're really not that special. They're average. I don't know why they want to see them." Laughing, she added, "Someday I might bare all my goodies as a last-ditch resort to revive my career. But I want to save it. I want to have my ace in the bag."

Halle's ace was ready to come out of the bag.

"I hate love scenes in which the woman's naked and the man's wearing a three-piece suit. I mean, fair's fair."

—Julia Roberts

"The truest cliché about Hollywood is that women have boobs and everybody wants to see them."

—Halle Berry

NINE

Monster

The enormous night had come at last. Now it was just the two of them. There were others there of course. The crew, which had been reduced to a skeleton. Her husband, who wasn't there in body, but who was never far from her mind. His wife, who has visited the set before disappearing like a ghost. But it was really just the two of them now. This had been building for three weeks. In the abstract, it had been somewhat frightening, somewhat intimidating; in the script, the scene had been raw, animalistic. She had never done a scene like this before and neither had he. And they had certainly never done anything like this together before. They didn't even know each other when shooting began. Now they were going to do something that, in many ways, was more intimate than sex. It was more intimate because it would be public: The whole world, or the audience for an indie film anyway, would be watching. It was more intimate because it was film, and it would last forever. And it was more intimate because they would do it again and again, throughout the enormous night, until they got it right. So now it began: skin on skin, chest to chest, tongue to tongue, grinding, moaning, sweating, letting go, all under the lights, with the skeleton crew watching, but the two of them were the only ones there. And they had never even kissed before.

It started without Halle, a *Monster* looking for a home. In 2000, shortly after *American Beauty* had dominated the Oscars, manager/producer Lee Daniels got a call. It was Sean Penn on the line, with a major proposal. Deals this big and interesting didn't typically come Daniels' way. As one of the few black producers in Hollywood, Daniels was a bit of an outsider. In fact, he was a lot of an outsider—he didn't even live in Hollywood. His offices were in New York City, so he could better maintain his perspective on the industry. Daniels only had one screen credit to his name—an acting part as "Steve, Mark's best friend" in the 1986 movie *A Little Off Mark*—but he was hungry and he was ready. He considered himself a man of the streets—his father, a police officer, was killed in the line of duty when Daniels was thirteen years old, leaving his mother to raise him in West Philadelphia by herself—and by scrapping and scraping he had managed to cobble together a fairly solid list of clients over the years. At one time or another he had managed Morgan Freeman, Amber Valletta, and Loretta Devine *(Waiting to Exhale* and TV's *Boston Public)*. But Daniels was more than ready to expand. He wanted to produce feature films.

Sean Penn had something else in mind. Here was his pitch: He was going to direct a new movie. This project was racially charged—it was about a black woman who falls for a racist white prison guard. It was going to push some buttons, raise some eyebrows, shake things up. Penn already had two other actors lined up: Robert De Niro was lined up to play the racist corrections officer and Marlon Brando was positioned to play the officer's even more racist father.

Daniels was excited. This was just the kind of film he wanted to get involved in. So what was his role supposed to be? Turned out, Penn didn't want him to produce; Penn wanted to sign on one of his clients. He had called to look into Wes Bentley's availability and interest in the movie. Bentley, who was only in his early twenties, was hot right now; his performance as Ricky Fitts, the troubled teenaged son of a closeted violent father in *American Beauty*, had gotten him noticed by studios all over Los Angeles—he was basically that season's "It" boy. Daniels expressed his client's interest. Penn told him the name of the movie: *Monster's Ball.* Months went by. "The project never got set up at a studio," Daniels would tell me later. "It never happened."

A year went by. Daniels was still shopping for good projects—for his clients and for himself. He didn't see a whole lot of good films out there that were exploring racial issues with any kind of intelligence and depth, and he wanted to change that. In the back of his mind he was still thinking about *Monster's Ball.* It was a great script. There was something real there. That was just the kind of project he needed to break out. He wondered what had happened to it.

Not long afterward Daniels got another call. This time it was Oliver Stone. The man who had made *Platoon* and *Wall Street* and *J.F.K.* and *Born on the Fourth of July* and *Natural Born Killers* was looking to rabble-rouse once again. Stone wanted to make *Monster's Ball.* This time around, other actors were connected to the project: Tommy Lee Jones was supposed to play the racist prison guard. It all sounded great to Daniels. "Let's do it," Daniels said. Weeks went by. Months went by. The film never happened.

Daniels decided to try to set up the film himself. "I said forget this," Daniels told me. "I'm calling the writers."

So he called them. Turned out the writers were frustrated as well. Writer number one, Milo Addica, was a first-timer looking to get something in production. Writer number two, Will Rokos, only had one screen credit to his name—and it wasn't even a writing one, it was a role as a Pie Vendor in a 1988 movie called *Galactic Gigolo.* They had been peddling *Monster's Ball* since 1995 and, despite all the stars who had become attached and unattached to the script, the project still hadn't found a home. But despite Daniels's interest, they needed some convincing. The writers appreciated Daniels's enthusiasm, but they weren't certain if they could trust him. Why did he, Lee Daniels, think he could get this controversial movie made when Sean Penn, Oliver Stone, and a bunch of other more famous, more powerful people had tried and failed?

Daniels figured the difference was that he was from West Philadelphia: He had scraped. He was scrappy. He could get it done. The writers gave him three months to try.

Nudity. Halle didn't want any part of movies that were about that. She had been passing on movies that had explicit sex scenes since she had gotten into showbiz. They had tried to get her to flash her "goodies" (as she called them) in *The Last Boy Scout* (1991) and she had refused, even though it was written in her contract, even though she needed the job, even though Bruce Willis and Damon Wayans were her co-stars. They hired a body double and it all worked out. She had made an exception for *Swordfish,* but that was all about personal growth, about seeing how far she could push herself. Plus, her husband had approved the scene, even encouraged it—and it was only a few seconds long. And besides, she had made $2.5 million off that film.

Now Halle had been slipped a script for this new project, *Monster's Ball.* By page thirty she wanted in. The characters were complex and yet somehow simple; they led harsh hard lives, but it was almost because they were imperfect that they were so sympathetic. And what a story: a waitress in the South named Leticia (the role she wanted) was raising an overweight son alone because her husband was on death row. After her son dies in an accident, she falls in love with a helpful stranger, a prison guard named Hank. Turns out Hank is a reformed racist who just happens to be one of the guards who was involved in the execution of Letitia's husband. The movie ended with a graphic scene of carnal release in which Letitia and Hank drop their prejudices, their inhibitions, their preconceptions, and even their clothes and engage in a wild, animalistic session of lovemaking. What was that quote from *Bulworth,* the movie she co-starred in with Warren Beatty back in 1998? "All we need is a voluntary, free-spirited, open-ended program of procreative racial deconstruction. Everybody just gotta keep fuckin' everybody till they're all the same color." That's what this movie was about—and it was about guilt and redemption and forgiveness, too. Halle wanted in.

Meanwhile, Daniels was looking for just the right director. He wanted someone who would come in with no preconceptions about the themes of the piece, no myths or baggage about the culture of the South and interracial relationships. He wanted someone who was unencumbered. "I wanted someone who would tell the story from a completely naive perspective," he told me.

So Daniels looked to Europe for the answer and he found Marc Forster, a young, thirtysomething director who was born in Germany but grew up in Switzerland. His résumé was light—he had previously directed only two films, *Loungers* (1995), a picture about a two-bit lounge singer that took home the audience award at Slamdance, the anti-Sundance film festival, and *Everything Put Together* (2000), a film about a suburban couple struggling unsuccessfully to deal with the death of their infant baby from sudden infant death syndrome (SIDS). Neither picture was ever distributed but both played the festival circuit, marking Forster as a scraper and a scrapper, just like Daniels. *Everything Put Together* was shot in just two weeks on a small Sony VX-1000 digital camera for just $100,000. This was Daniels's kind of guy.

Next Daniels went to line up a studio. He always saw himself as a man with a lot of connections—he moved across social strata pretty freely, so he knew people: black and white, famous and unknown, rich and poor. He was only a few degrees of separation away from anyone in Hollywood. So for *Monster's Ball* he wanted payback; it was time to call in favors. He began to see studio executives and the like, but couldn't get any commitments, couldn't line up any money. "I tapped various friends," Daniels told me. "I thought someone would give me a break, but they wouldn't." After every meeting, after every no, after every good-bye handshake, Daniels would say this by way of parting: "I will see you at the Oscars."

Finally, Daniels caught a break. He had got Billy Bob Thornton *(Sling Blade)* attached to the project and it was now generating buzz—and new interest. The indie studio Lions Gate agreed to back the production. Lions Gate was a new outfit (chairman Frank Giustra founded it in 1997) but it was successful in a modest but critically acclaimed way. Over its short existence, its roster of productions included *Buffalo 66* (a quirky comedy helmed by Vincent Gallo), *Eve's Bayou* (a drama starring Samuel L. Jackson and directed by a black female filmmaker, Kasi Lemmons), and *Amores Perros* (a thrilling Mexican film that nabbed the fledgling studio a foreign-language film Oscar nomination).

So Daniels signed on to Lions Gate. There was one problem: He could only get $3.5 million to make the picture. Not a penny more. Take it or leave it. Daniels took it. He knew now he was going to have to work fast and cheap.

Nobody wanted Halle Berry. She and her manager had been pestering Daniels and his director for weeks about *Monster's Ball*. Daniels didn't want to see her. Every black actress in Hollywood, it seemed, wanted this role, and he wanted someone who looked the part, who had gravitas, who wasn't Hollywood. They already had Billy Bob Thornton and Wes Bentley. Now all they needed was the right Letitia. Halle and her representative kept calling. Her manager somehow got the director's number and badgered him about Halle for twenty minutes.

Finally beaten down by all the calls, Daniels gave Halle's representative an ultimatum: "The only way Halle Berry can come in for this," he said, "is if she's not Halle Berry."

So Daniels agreed to meet with Halle at Shutters, a hotel in Santa Monica. Halle came in to meet him—and she looked stunning. The curves. The super-cute short hair. The perfect smile. The golden skin. The almost relentless air of affability. The twinkling eyes. She was a vision of loveliness, one of the true screen beauties in

Hollywood. Halle Berry had come in looking exactly like Halle Berry. Unfortunately, the part called for an everyday waitress facing everyday problems in the Deep South. Bad skin. Bad hair. Dead eyes. No smiles. Daniels let Halle have it right off: "Listen," said Daniels, "you're simply not right for this. You're too beautiful for the role."

Now, one of Halle's great acting gifts—and she has many—is the ability to really nail a great tell-off scene. Bette Davis was a master at it—in *All About Eve* (1950) she cuts into Gary Merrill with the precision of a heart surgeon. Julia Roberts is another expert at the craft, knocking Aaron Eckhart to the turf in *Erin Brockovich* (2000). Halle, over her career, has told off Eddie Murphy in *Boomerang* ("Love should have brought your ass home last night!"), Jessica Lange in *Losing Isaiah* ("Look in the mirror. Look at my face. I'm his mother. God says so"), and her manager in *Introducing Dorothy Dandridge* ("When exactly did you protect me—when I was peeing in the cup or when they were draining the pool?"). There is an art to the tell-off; it can't be simply shrill. It must dress down a character even as it builds up an argument; it releases a particular power in an actress, allowing them to use brains, not brawn, to get their way on screen.

So Halle told off Daniels: "Who are you to tell me I'm too beautiful for this role?" she said. Many women, if not most, if not the overwhelming majority of actresses, would accept the adjective of "beautiful" as a compliment. But Halle had heard it too many times before, and every time such a compliment was paid, someone was trying to take something from her. She was told she was "too beautiful" to play a crackhead in *Jungle Fever*. She was told she was "too attractive" to play a poor mom who had lost her kid in *Losing Isaiah*. She won those roles, but she had lost others because producers and directors took one look at her and slid her into a category: "Too pretty." "Too black." "Not black enough." "Not for us."

So she let Daniels have it. The character in *Monster's Ball* was a working-class woman, a woman down on her luck, down on her life. Why *couldn't* she be beautiful? Was Daniels implying that the poor were ugly, that they looked different from other people, that they had to conform to a certain type? Didn't he have relatives who were working poor, or down on their luck, or perhaps even on drugs? Weren't some of them pretty? Said Halle, "What makes you think this woman has to look a certain way?"

Even as Halle laid into him, something subtle was going on, Daniels realized. He realized right off that she had a point. He *did* have relatives who were poor and pretty—to make such things mutually exclusive was wrongheaded. Every black person was pretty much, in his view, a generation from the ghetto—all sorts of blacks fit into all sorts of categories, just like any other kind of people. But there was something else going on, as Halle continued to argue: *She was making her points in character.* Even as she was arguing for herself in the role, she was *playing* the role, showing she had the forcefulness and toughness to carry it off.

In *Introducing Dorothy Dandridge,* Halle performed a scene in which Dandridge wins the lead role in *Carmen Jones* by arriving at the director's office dressed as Carmen, with a red rose and tight black dress. Now Halle was doing something similar, becoming a character to convince a filmmaker she was the one. Daniels didn't need any more convincing. Halle was the one. Not long afterward, the director and the studio were on board as well. Halle was paid $100,000 for her part.

After all her expenses, she would say later, she cleared about $5,000.

The shoot was like how sex sometimes is: short, fast, and hard. Wes Bentley fell ill and a few days before shooting he was replaced by rising Aussie hunk Heath Ledger *(The Patriot). Monster's Ball* was filmed in New Orleans. The temperatures were hot, the locations—prisons, bars, houses—were sometimes difficult and cramped. One barkeep temporarily blocked the crew from shooting because the script had swear words in it. Real prison guards were recruited to play some of the guards in the movie. Every day was a race to beat the sun, to outpace the clock, to get the good light before the sky went dark. They had twenty-five days to film a motion picture. The race was on.

There wasn't much money—actually, there pretty much was *no* money—for amenities. "We had bubble-gum and Popsicle sticks—that was the foundation of the film," Daniels told me. Some days Halle did her own makeup. Some days Sean "Puffy" Combs, who played

Halle's husband, helped move furniture on the set. Thornton cracked jokes before almost every take—often on off-color subjects like Preparation-H and rectal tissue and the like. Sometimes he would break into his drawling *Sling Blade* character, breaking up the cast and crew. Halle, who likes to focus before a scene, would sometimes go into a closet to escape all the hilarity before an emotional scene. Daniels, who had negotiated the color of a phone in an actor's trailer on other films in which he had a connection, was pleasantly surprised by the way people came together. It was like doing community theater, except with cameras.

One of the final sequences shot was the sex scene. On screen, it runs for about three minutes. To create it, the team filmed all night—around five hours. Halle felt almost as if she had been dating Thornton during the shoot, getting a feel for him, getting to know him. Before she met him, she didn't get the talk that he was sexy. Now that she had spent some time with him, she felt the pull and thought that there was an almost indescribable sexiness about him—and the very fact that it was indefinable was what made it so intriguing. She was ready for the scene. The filmmakers decided they wanted to wait until dark, until the sun was setting. Most of the crew was cleared out, leaving only a few key members. Daniels, in order to create an uninhibited atmosphere for his leads, struck an extraordinary bargain with them: He gave them the right to oversee the sex scene. If they didn't like any of the shots that were used, they could veto them. And Daniels had it written into Halle's and Thornton's contracts that if they didn't like the sex scene, if they weren't comfortable with it, the film couldn't be released.

Most sex scenes in movies are as carefully planned out as shuttle launches. Every position, every kiss, every stroke is negotiated, agreed to, choreographed. No actress wants an actor improvising a feel or a French kiss or something more intimate. But because Halle and Thornton had the final say on their scene, the rulebook was thrown out. They didn't worry about what the camera was catching because they knew they were in control. Sharon Stone once charged that the director of her breakthrough movie *Basic Instinct,* Paul Verhoeven, had positioned a camera to show her crotch in the notorious interrogation scene and that she had no idea she was revealing so much. Halle and Thornton wouldn't have that problem. They could reveal all and still reveal nothing.

Later, Halle screened the film for her husband, Eric. It was a private screening, just the two of them. She wanted him to see the film before the world did. After the sex scene, Eric stood up.

"I'll be right back," he said to Halle.

Not long afterward, he returned to his seat.

"Okay, I can continue now," he said.

After the movie was finished, Eric explained his feelings to Halle.

"You know, it was worth it and I'm so proud of you," he said. "I don't know if America's gonna get it. I don't know what will happen with it, but I'm proud of you that you took that risk and that you really . . . you really went there."

In *Monster's Ball* Halle Berry gives a performance for the ages. Many big stars have problems working with kids—like real stars, they suck everything small into their gravitational orbit. Halle, in her scenes with her overweight son, shows nuance and empathy, even as she plays a woman who is disgusted and confused and full of rage over her son's behavior and by the dissolution of her marriage. Many big stars also have trouble playing ordinary, nonglamorous, working-class folks. Their everyday mannerisms are too big, too showy, and are obviously only for the cameras. Halle seems to channel all the pissed-off rage she has about her own career into her role as Leticia. She never plays it big, she keeps it subtle and buried, like real life.

The performances in *Monster's Ball* are all first rate. The one place the movie is lacking is in its theme: The basic plot about a black woman falling in love with the white racist murderer of her husband seems to be a segregationist's fantasy. The movie creates a world in which a man who has let racism rule his life is able to switch gears, without apology or explanation, and bed down the best-looking black woman in town. Mysteriously, a helpful neighbor (played by rapper Mos Def) is never considered as a possible love interest for Halle. It's also telling that Halle's executed husband is played by another rapper, Sean "Puffy" Combs. It's almost as if the movie is trying to soothe American fears of hip-hop by killing and neutering back rappers cinematically and replacing them with white racists.

In families—or churches—in which there is child

abuse, one of the biggest problems is silence. Abusers always want to move on, let the past be the past, perhaps pay off a civil suit and get on with their lives. In *Monster's Ball,* Hank never apologizes for his actions, never explains his change of heart, never even tells Halle's character that he was the one who executed her husband. Instead, he pays her off—naming a store after her, fixing her car, and giving her a place to stay. She moves in with him, at least at first, for economic reasons, not for love. How can we believe Hank is redeemed? In court, when someone pleads guilty to something, they must admit to their crimes. Hanks never does that. There can't be any redemption without explanation.

And yet Halle gives the film its beating heart. The acclaim she won for this role was richly deserved. As the daughter of a black father and a white mother, she knows, firsthand, the barriers and prejudice that interracial love faces. As a young girl whose home was filled with violence, she's felt the sting of child abuse. One looks at her in close-up in this movie and realizes, if one hasn't before, that set in her pretty face are haunted eyes. Her eyes are as sad as broken windows on a boarded-up house. She reaches past glamour and glitz and stereotype in *Monster's Ball* and pulls up pure pain.

James Baldwin, in his 1976 book *The Devil Finds Work,* wrote that "not one [black American actor] has ever been seriously challenged to deliver the best that is in him." Halle hasn't waited for a call, she's gone out and won her roles; she hasn't simply relied on a script, she finds emotional depths that aren't on the page. She set her own goals and faced challenges worthy of her gifts.

Combs, for one, was impressed by Halle's on-set focus. As a newcomer to acting, as a man who gained fame as a music producer and rapper, Combs thought he'd be the most focused performer on the set, because he had the most to learn and the most to lose. But to Combs, the level of intensity Halle brought to her role was almost frightening. Every day, for every shot, Combs would tell reporters later, Halle seemed to *be* her character, she *was* Leticia. But what was perhaps even more noteworthy was the fact that, even as she buried herself in her performance, the caring Halle, the friendly Halle, the collegial Halle, would sometimes poke her way through, as needed. When a scene with Combs went well, Halle would acknowledge it with a "Good job." Acting can be a kind of autistic profession, with its practitioners caught up in the hermetically sealed vagaries of the craft. Halle always maintains that cordial, emotional connection with the people she works with. It brings a warmth to her acting that many other fine actors just don't have.

Monster's Ball was a huge hit in relation to its cost, and the biggest smash ever for its studio, Lions Gate. It grossed $31 million in the United States alone; its British gross alone (the equivalent of some $3 million) would have been enough to cover its production costs.

Now Halle's daring was finally going to get rewarded with something more important than money.

"For me, as for the mass of Negro women,
there was this enormous and well-defined barrier.
God, if God were a beautiful black woman,
probably couldn't surmount it."

—DOROTHY DANDRIDGE

"Will tonight change the industry? I don't know.
But if it changes the minds of those people who felt
defeated, if now they feel hopeful, eventually those
inspired hearts will make a change. I believe that."

—HALLE BERRY

TEN

And the Oscar Goes to . . .

She had played this scene before. In another life, in another movie. She knew how this movie ended, she had seen the credits roll. But that was acting. That was someone else's life. This was her life. She would live it for real this time. God couldn't help her. She believed in a higher power of some sort, but she was not a regular churchgoer. Sometimes she felt Catholic, other times Baptist, other times interdenominational. But God couldn't help her now. She had dreamed what it would be like to stand up there, before all her peers, and hold the highest award her profession had to give. In some hidden part of her, she longed to slam everybody who had ever screwed her over. The list would be long. But she'd never do that. She'd rather just say: You know who you are. Maybe she'd never get the chance. Maybe, on this night of nights, she'd never get up there at all. She'd played that scene before, too.

The odds were against her.

It wasn't just a cliché. It wasn't just race-talk based on Hollywood's track record when it came to race. It wasn't just because her film, *Monster's Ball,* was super-low budget and her studio, Lions Gate, wasn't exactly a major.

Las Vegas bookmakers said the odds were against her. Halle, in the category of actress in a leading role, was up against Nicole Kidman for *Moulin Rouge* (sympathy vote—she had just broken up with hubby Tom Cruise), Sissy Spacek for *In the Bedroom* (comeback vote—Hollywood loves rediscovering a veteran/survivor), Renee Zellweger in *Bridget Jones' Diary* (a wildcard vote—it was a comedy, which was a minus for Oscar, but the studio was award-savvy Miramax and Zellweger faked a nice British accent for the part, both pluses), and Judi Dench for *Iris* (another wildcard vote—nobody saw the film but they might vote based on Dench's stellar acting rep). In February 2002, Bally's-Paris hotel-casino sports book picked Kidman at 2–1 to win the prize and Halle at just 6–1, tied with Dench; Caesars Palace put Kidman and Spacek at 5–2 odds with Halle behind.

March 24, 2002: When Halle arrived at the new Kodak Theatre in Los Angeles, where the awards were being held for the first time, she already looked like a winner. Sandra Bullock and Sharon Stone had made the scene dressed in basic black; Kidman had shown up in a frilly pink frock that washed out her already wan appearance; Jennifer Connelly, who can be a stunner, had pulled up in a droopy dress that seemed to make her chest wilt with shame. Halle, in a wine-colored dress with a see-through floral-patterned bodice, looked like a movie star—elegant and sexy, daring and yet with crisp, classic curves. Her dress was designed by Elie Saab; Halle could have gone with a more established designer, like Valentino, one of her favorites, but she wanted something fresh, and she wanted to give a new fashionista a chance. The dress was actually more risqué when she first saw it, but she had more embroidery and appliqués added to the upper half to make it less revealing. The media consensus was that Halle was the stunner of the night. The cameras flashed as she walked the red carpet with her husband, Eric Benet. It must have reminded Halle of the scene she had fought for—and then paid for—in *Introducing Dorothy Dandridge*.

She had indeed played this scene before.

The night before, at a gathering at Mirabelle, a club on Sunset Boulevard in West Hollywood, black Hollywood had turned out to give her their best wishes. The party was sponsored by Lions Gate, Revlon (Halle was their spokesperson), and Halle's manager. Oprah was there. Samuel L. Jackson was there. Angela Bassett was there. Louis Gossett Jr. was there. They'd all been nominated for Oscars in the past and they'd all lost. Halle was carrying all their dreams, although Bassett would reveal later that she had mixed feelings about Halle's Oscar run. Oprah told Halle: "My heart is beating for you."

But as Halle glided to her seat on Oscar day, she knew she was facing an uphill struggle. No black woman in the history of the Academy Awards had ever won a best actress Oscar. Only two had won supporting

Oscars—Hattie McDaniel in 1939 for her role as a slave mammy in *Gone With the Wind* (after she won, Olivia de Havilland, who was up for the same award for the same movie, dissolved into frustrated tears and had to be escorted to the kitchen), and Whoopi Goldberg for her comic turn in *Ghost* in 1990. Seventy-three years. No best actress.

Lee Daniels, producer of *Monster's Ball,* said Halle grew strangely quiet in the days leading up to the Oscars. Davis himself had gone on CNN predicting a win, but he says even as he said it, "In my heart of hearts I knew it was total b.s. I didn't think she was really going to win. History speaks for itself. I thought that maybe Denzel [Washington, nominated for best actor for *Training Day*] would win, just so they could say they did the right thing by black folks. But I didn't think she was going to win." After all, Halle and *Monster's Ball* were on a losing roll in the post-season acting awards—Halle had been nominated for AFI Actor of the Year Female but lost out to Spacek; she had been nominated for a Golden Globe for best performance by an actress in a motion picture drama but she lost out again to Spacek; she even lost at the MTV Movie Awards—she was up for best female performance, but Nicole Kidman grabbed the prize. Halle had won a Screen Actors Guild Award, but that was just one win out of many losses. Daniels had asked Halle how she was doing not long before the Oscars. "Traumatized," was her reply.

Seventy-three years. No best actress. The Academy Awards has a history of traumatizing black women—as well as black men, minorities in general, and women (and, frankly, white male stars, too). The first Academy Awards were held May 16, 1929, in the Blossom Room of the Hollywood Roosevelt Hotel. Right from the start, the worth of the award and the integrity of the process were scrutinized and questioned. Douglas Fairbanks, the president of the Academy, said around the time of the first awards: "It is a bit like asking, 'Does this man play checkers better than that man plays chess?'" The very first Oscar ever, for best actor, went to Emil Jannings, a Swiss-born silent film star who became Hitler's "first actor" and an integral part of the Nazi film industry. Jannings had left Hollywood for Berlin before the ceremony and so the statuette was given to him in advance and he carried it back with him to Germany. After World War II, Jannings played down his support of the Nazis, telling reporters he had to "go along with Hitler or be sent to a concentration camp." But there's no arguing what he did: During the war years he enthusiastically accepted an offer from Nazi propaganda chief Joseph Goebbels to appear in pro-German, anti-Semitic films. After the war, he was a film pariah and died of cancer in 1950 in Austria. When a real-life Nazi is Oscar's first winner, what chance did Halle have?

Oscar's diversity track record over the years has not been good. Spike Lee—the man who kick-started the African-American film boom of the nineties, the film-maker whose films, including *Do the Right Thing*, *Jungle Fever*, and *Malcolm X*, were among the most dynamic in this history of American cinema—has *never* been nominated for a best director Oscar. In fact, only one black filmmaker has ever been nominated for best director—John Singleton for *Boyz N the Hood* (1991).

Every black woman, up to Halle Berry, who had ever been nominated for lead actress lost, including Dandridge for *Carmen Jones* (1954), Diana Ross for *Lady Sings the Blues* (1972), Cicely Tyson for *Sounder* (1972), Diahann Carroll for *Claudine* (1974), Whoopi Goldberg for *The Color Purple* (1985), and Angela Bassett for *What's Love Got to Do With It* (1993).

No black woman had been nominated for lead actress twice. You got one shot and it was over. It should also be noted that in its entire history, only two women have received best director nominations—Jane Campion for *The Piano* (1993) and Lina Wertmuller for *Seven Beauties* (1976). In 1992, *The Prince of Tides* was nominated for best actor, best actress, best cinematography, best art direction, best music, best screenplay, best picture—pretty much everything but best catering—but the director, Barbra Streisand, was passed over for a nomination in her category. She was gracious about being snubbed, telling the *Los Angeles Times* that "there are a lot of good movies in contention," but she also added that sexism was a problem in the industry. "It's as if a man were allowed to have passion and commitment to his work, but a woman is allowed that feeling for a man, but not her work."

Seventy-three years. No best actress. Halle had her work cut out for her.

• • •

In 1954, Dorothy Dandridge became the first black woman ever nominated in the category of best actress at the Oscars. The nod was for her role in *Carmen Jones*. Before the ceremony, the director of the movie, Otto Preminger, gave her his opinion bluntly, and delivered it as if it were cold fact.

"You will not get the Oscar," Preminger told her.

"Why not?" Dandridge answered.

"The time is not ripe."

Dandridge was nervous before the ceremony, but by all accounts she was all style, all beauty. The Associated Press reported afterward: "Dorothy Dandridge is a picture of loveliness as she attends the Academy Awards presentations at New York's Century Theater. The gracious Dandridge stole the show at New York's version of the Academy Award ceremonies though movie stars and celebrities were a dime a dozen." According to the book *Dorothy Dandridge,* by her manager, Earl Mills, Dandridge was petrified with fright as she waited backstage. After all, her competition consisted of Hollywood's most stunning and well-known women: Judy Garland *(A Star Is Born)*, Audrey Hepburn *(Sabrina)*, Grace Kelly *(The Country Girl)*, and Jane Wyman *(The Magnificent Obsession)*. They were all at the ceremonies (there was also a matching one being held at Pantages Theatre in Hollywood), except for Garland, who had just given birth (NBC-TV cameras were positioned outside her hospital room on a special scaffold in case she won).

The night was turning into a big sweep for *On the Waterfront,* starring Marlon Brando. The film would take eight awards that night, including best actor for the young Brando.

William Holden strode onto the stage; time was short so he didn't even read the nominees. He just announced the winner: Grace Kelly for *The Country Girl.*

Dorothy said to her manager: "I wish Judy had won it." Brando came over and kissed her. A few people buzzed about that—an interracial kiss at the Oscars. It turned out to be her good-bye kiss. Dandridge was never nominated again; what's more, despite her talents, she never even landed a part that would be worthy of a nomination.

The 2002 Academy Awards featured a look back at film history in the person of Sidney Poitier. It was a sweet convergence: Washington and Halle were up for lead actor Oscars on the same night that the last black lead actor winner—the only black lead Oscar winner—was being honored.

Poitier put his years of struggle into words: "I arrived in Hollywood at the age of twenty-two in a time different than today's, a time in which the odds against my standing here tonight fifty-three years later would not have fallen in my favor. Back then, no route had been established for where I was hoping to go, no pathway left in evidence for me to trace, no custom for me to follow.

"Yet here I am this evening at the end of a journey that in 1949 would have been considered almost impossible, and in fact might never have been set in motion were there not an untold number of courageous, unselfish choices made by a handful of visionary American filmmakers, directors, writers, and producers; each with a strong sense of citizenship responsibility to the times in which they lived; each unafraid to permit their art to reflect their views and values, ethical and moral, and moreover, acknowledge them as their own. They knew the odds that stood against them and their efforts were overwhelming and likely could have proven too high to overcome. Still, those filmmakers persevered, speaking through their art to the best in all of us. And I've benefited from their effort. The industry benefited from their effort. America benefited from their effort. And in ways large and small the world has also benefited from their effort."

He concluded by saying: "I accept this award in memory of all the African-American actors and actresses who went before me in the difficult years, on whose shoulders I was privileged to stand to see where I might go."

There was a montage of current movie actors praising Poitier shown before his speech—all the actors in it seemed to be black (if there were any whites, if you blinked, you missed them). That same night, Robert Redford was also honored for his work—his montage consisted entirely of *white* actors praising his work (if there were any minorities, if you blinked, you missed them).

Hollywood, it seemed, was still living in separate and unequal worlds.

• • •

Halle's big moment was fast approaching. Daniels, who had been sitting with the writers for *Monster's Ball* (they had been nominated for best screenplay, but lost) went up to Halle's seat to check on her. She seemed jumpy. Weird. Out of sorts.

Daniels asked her, "What's going on?"

She replied: "This is bigger than me. This is not about you, Lee, and this is not about me. We can't lose this."

The enormity of the moment had finally hit her. She had made a movie about a woman who had simply been nominated—just nominated!—and almost fifty years later it was still a legendary loss. Almost fifty years later nobody had completed the journey that Dandridge began. What if Halle won? What would that mean? Would they still be talking about it fifty years from now? A hundred years from now? After all, there had been a seventy-three-year-long wait already. And, so far, still no wins for black actresses in a leading role.

Daniels noticed that Halle's knees were shaking. He wanted to say something to bolster her, show his support. He looked her in the eye. He wanted to say something to her but he didn't want to say it too loud because Sissy Spacek was sitting literally two feet away. He leaned in close.

Daniels told her: "Halle, we're gonna take this mother-f——ker home tonight."

At that, Halle laughed—at the bluntness of it, at the streetiness of it.

Then Halle got serious again. She went back to looking weird.

"We need to win this for our people," she said.

Daniels was frightened by the look on her face, by the possibility of failure. He thought: "We're going to lose." But he put on his best producer's smile and then turned away. As soon as his back was turned, he put on a "psychotic" frown.

He now felt the way Halle looked: weird.

The moment arrived. Russell Crowe prepared to announce the winner in the category of best actress. It had been the roughest Oscar race in history. There had been charges that Berry, Washington, and Will Smith (nominated for lead actor for *Ali*) had been playing the race card. Julia Roberts went public saying that Washington deserved to win. There had been stories suggesting the filmmakers behind *A Beautiful Mind* were homophobic and perhaps insensitive to Jewish concerns because they left out incidents from the book that was the source of their biopic of schizophrenic mathematician John Nash that detailed sexual encounters he had with other men, and that he had also expressed anti-Semitic sentiments.

It was also the most expensive Oscar race in history. By some estimates, Universal, the studio behind *A Beautiful Mind*, spent $15 million or more in their Oscar campaign—or $2,600 for each of the 5,739 voting Academy members. Some rival studios had spent more money courting Oscar voters than Lions Gate had spent to *make* their film. Individual Academy members were having more money spent to court them by all the various studios than Halle Berry had cleared in making *Monster's Ball.*

And now Crowe read the winner for lead actress. And the Oscar goes to: Halle Berry.

Everyone saw Halle's reaction. She looked as if a hurricane had knocked her over in her seat. You had to wonder if she could get up, if she could speak, if she could master her senses.

Daniels, in the audience, can only remember this: "Screaming and hollering and screaming and hollering." He wondered if he heard it right. Then he went back to screaming and hollering and screaming and hollering.

Martha Coolidge, who had directed Halle to an Emmy in *Dorothy Dandridge,* was also watching. She told me afterward: "I was in the audience. I was there. I actually had a feeling she would win. Where I got the feeling was at the SAG [Screen Actors Guild] Awards earlier. When she won the SAG Award I felt she really had a shot at winning the Oscar. No particular reason outside the fact that there are an enormous number of actors who are members of the Academy. It just meant people in the industry had seen the movie and had voted for her. . . . Because I worked on *Introducing Dorothy Dandridge,* I know how significant her win is to a whole community of people. Halle wanted to carry on. And she has carried on because she won. It's amazing, in only two years the dream came true—the dream of carrying on in Dorothy's footsteps. The dream of Halle's was to give the woman who broke the barriers back to the public and to be offered opportunities herself. What happened in fact is that she carried on from where Dorothy left off and has gone farther."

Warrington Hudlin, who produced Halle's first big-budget film, *Boomerang*, was watching from the Tribeca Grand in New York City: "I leaped—I must have leaped two feet off the floor," he told me later. "It was very cathartic, because I knew how talented this woman is. But we also know talent is not enough. But the stars aligned, so there you go."

Amy Holden Jones, director of *The Rich Man's Wife*, was overjoyed at her former leading lady's win. Jones told me: "I was watching her and jumping up and down and screaming. It was certainly a wonderful historical moment. But I was more relating to the personal triumph. Her emotions played so beautifully on her face, to see her so overcome, you just wanted to put your arms around her and hug her. At the same time, what a great thing. I kept thinking: For the rest of her life, she's always going to have this. It's the kind of thing that you realize your obituary's going to lead off: the first black actress to win the Oscar. It's pretty amazing." She went on: "The other thing I felt when I saw her Oscar win: seeing her hold out her hand to her husband. I thought how marvelous that she's found that kind of love and happiness now."

Robert Townsend, in an essay in *Razor* magazine, said that "I thought to myself 'Man, this is beautiful.' I've worked with Halle—I directed her in the comedy *B.A.P.S.*—during a time when she was going through a storm in her life; when her divorce from David Justice was brand spanking new. . . . So when she got emotional and choked up, I knew why." Townsend added, "It may be another seventy-four years before it happens again, like Halley's Comet."

When Halle took the podium (Russell Crowe told her to "Breathe mate. Just breathe. It's going to be okay."), there were tears streaming down her face. She somehow found her voice and the words, like her tears, gushed out of her: "Oh, my God. Oh, my God. I'm sorry. This moment is so much bigger than me. This moment is for Dorothy Dandridge, Lena Horne, Diahann Carroll. It's for the women that stand beside me, Jada Pinkett, Angela Bassett, Vivica Fox. And it's for every nameless, faceless woman of color that now has a chance because this door tonight has been opened. Thank you. I'm so honored. I'm so honored. And I thank the Academy for choosing me to be the vessel for which His blessing might flow."

Halle went on, gaining a bit more composure and pausing to run through the Oscar ritual of thanks. Said Halle: "I want to thank my manager, Vincent Cirrincione. He's been with me for twelve long years and you fought every fight and you loved me when I've been up, but more importantly you've loved me when I've been down. You have been a manager, a friend, and the only father I've ever known. Really. And I love you very much. I want to thank my mom who has given me the strength to fight every single day, to be who I want to be and to give me the courage to dream, that this dream might be happening and possible for me. I love you, Mom, so much. Thank you my husband, who is just a joy of my life, and India, thank you for giving me peace because only with the peace that you've brought me have I been allowed to go to places that I never even knew I could go. Thank you. I love you and India with all my heart."

Halle's Oscar night Thanksgiving continued: "I want to thank Lions Gate. Thank you. Mike Paseornek, Tom Ortenberg for making sure everybody knew about this little tiny movie. Thank you for believing in me. Our director Marc Forster, you're a genius. You're a genius. This movie-making experience was magical for me because of you. You believed in me, you trusted me, and you gently guided me to very scary places. I thank you. I want to thank Ivana Chubic, I could have never figured out who the heck this lady was without you. I love you. Thank you. I want to thank Lee Daniels, our producer. Thank you for giving me this chance, for believing that I could do it. And now tonight I have this. Thank you."

As she neared the end of her thanks, she finally felt the weight of time. A few minutes seemed too short to say all the things that needed to be said. Halle continued: "I want to thank my agents. CAA, Josh Lieberman especially. I have to thank my agents. Kevin Huvane, thank you. Thank you for never kicking me out and sending me somewhere else. Thank you. Um . . . I, I, I, who else? I have so many people that I know I need to thank. My lawyers! Neil Meyer, thank you. Okay, wait a minute. I got to take . . . seventy-four years here! I got to take this time! I got to thank my lawyer, Neil Meyer, for making this deal. Doug Stone. I need to thank lastly and not leastly, I have to thank Spike Lee for putting me in my very first film and believing in me. Oprah Winfrey for being the best role model any girl can have. Joel Silver, thank you. And thank you to Warren Beatty. Thank you so much for being my mentors and believing in me. Thank you! Thank you! Thank you!"

When she reached backstage, still overcome by her win and the moment, Washington said: "She's gone. She's not even with us right now."

But the night wasn't over yet. Far from it. Julia Roberts took the stage later. She had won the Oscar for best actress the year before for *Erin Brockovich* and was presenting the award for best actor. She tore open the envelope. "I love my life," she said, smiling. The winner was Denzel Washington, for *Training Day.* Roberts had starred opposite Washington in *The Pelican Brief* in 1993. She had championed him in the press for *Training Day.* Now she would get to had him an Oscar. In 1954, Marlon Brandon kissed Dorothy Dandridge when she lost and it caused a stir. In 2002, Roberts would kiss Washington when he won and nobody raised an eyebrow. The kiss denied her in *The Pelican Brief* she got to deliver in real life.

Washington—calm, cool, confident, his eyes dry and his bearing erect, found humor in the moment—and heart as well. Washington said: "Two birds in one night, huh? Oh, God is good. God is great. God is great. From the bottom of my heart, I thank you all. Forty years I've been chasing Sidney [Poitier], they finally give it to me, what'd they do? They give it to him the same night. I'll always be chasing you, Sidney. I'll always be following in your footsteps. There's nothing I would rather do, sir. Nothing I would rather do. God bless you. God bless you."

Washington, as composed as Halle had been emotional, went on: "I want to thank the Academy. You know, when I was in college first starting out as an actor, they asked each one of us what we wanted to do. I said I want to be the best actor in the world. All the students in the classroom looked at me like I was a nut. Life has taught me to just try and be the best that I can be, and I thank the Academy for saying to me that on this given night, I was the best that I could be. I want to thank Warner Brothers and Alan Horn and Lorenzo di Bonaventura for supporting this film. And Antoine Fuqua, a brilliant young filmmaker, African-American filmmaker. I don't know where you are, Antoine, love you. Ethan Hawke, my partner in crime. So many people, I can't even remember everybody, lawyers, doctors, agents . . . My beautiful agent, Ed Limato. We've been together for so many years. Hometown boy from Mount Vernon. My beautiful wife. I love you so much. You put up with me, in spite of myself. And my beautiful children at home. I told you if I lost tonight I would come home and we'd celebrate and if I won tonight I would come home and we'd celebrate. Well, I'm coming home, we're celebrating. God bless you all."

Sidney Poitier, after winning the best actor Oscar for *Lilies of the Field* (1963), could not find work. Not good work anyway.

The book *Oscar Dearest* by Peter H. Brown and Jim Pinkston, quotes Poitier's agent, Martin Baum, as saying that after the Oscar, the industry wrote the win off as a "onetime thing—unlikely to be repeated." Afterward, Poitier and his agent tried for months, unsuccessfully, to get funding for his next picture, *To Sir, With Love.* Nobody was interested. In the end, James Clavell agreed to write the script for basically nothing and to direct for a percentage of the profits. Said Baum: "Sidney had to work at no salary just to prove himself all over again— and that was all after the Oscar."

To Sir, With Love was one of the biggest hits of 1967, but it didn't receive a single Oscar nomination. Poitier was never nominated again. Said Poitier of his Oscar win: "The only real change in my career was in the attitude of newsmen. And they started to query me on civil rights and the Negro question incessantly. Ever since I won the Oscar, that's what they've been interested in— period."

Dandridge's career faltered after her Oscar nomination. In her autobiography, *Everything and Nothing,* she wrote that she believed that there was a limit to the kinds of parts she would be allowed to get from Hollywood. She believed, toward the end of her life, that Hollywood would allow her to play parts like Carmen in *Carmen Jones* and Bess in *Porgy and Bess* because those were "whore" parts, roles that were "wanton," characters who were out to simply score sex, and not full-bodied roles of women looking for husbands and lasting romance. Elizabeth Taylor, Marilyn Monroe,

Ava Gardener—they were all allowed to play such roles, but not her; even after her Oscar nomination, Dandridge was scrounging for parts just to pay her bills. She thought that once she had opened the world, it would remain open, but she discovered opportunity is a swinging door—ready to crush fingers, pin dreams in the doorjamb, and perhaps close and lock again, never to be reopened.

Dandridge wrote: "For me, as for the mass of Negro women, there was this enormous and well-defined barrier. God, if God were a beautiful black woman, probably couldn't surmount it."

Halle had a big night of celebration ahead of her. "I never thought this would be possible in my lifetime," Halle said backstage at the Oscar ceremonies. "I hope we will start to be judged on our merits and our work. This moment, it's not really just about me, it's about so many people that went before me. It's about people who are fighting alongside me, and now it will be indelibly easier. It's not about me, but about so many other women of color.

"Tonight means that every woman of color should be hopeful, because it can happen. And I hope that's what tonight brings. Will tonight change the industry? I don't know. But if it changes the minds of those people who felt defeated, if now they feel hopeful, eventually those inspired hearts will make a change. I believe that." She continued: "I had to fight for this, and now this is so worth it. I've got my mother here, my husband, my manager, and we are just going to party until noon tomorrow."

But a debate had begun: Had anyone really changed anything? "The wins that we saw on Oscar night are arguably well deserved—they gave some great performances," agent Rob Kim of United Talent Agency, one of only a very few Asian-American agents in Hollywood, told the *Los Angeles Times.* "I don't know that it necessarily matters that much. Does [Berry's] win mean more roles for African-American women? I don't think so. I think more people will want to hire Denzel and more people will want to hire Halle Berry."

After the big wins, Hudlin told me: "Part of me is extremely excited. But the veteran part of me says don't get carried away. The same people are still making decisions on what gets done. I can't allow myself to think that the industry has fundamentally changed, because it hasn't.

"The other thing that was not emphasized enough about that Oscar night was that the movie that Halle got the Oscar for was produced by a black filmmaker and the movie that Denzel got an Oscar for was directed by a black filmmaker. I think that's a very key thing—who is behind the camera calling the shots. Lee Daniels, who produced *Monster's Ball* and Antoine Fuqua, who directed *Training Day,* were not properly acknowledged by the media."

Halle herself soon came under fire. A few days after the Oscars, her official website, www.hallewood.com, was hacked into. A photo of her was vandalized—a mustache and a beard was drawn on. But on a more disturbing note, an e-mail address left by the cyber attacker contained three letters: KKK. Her site was pulled down briefly and the security upgraded.

A few months later, friendly fire was lobbed in. Angela Bassett reportedly told *Newsweek* magazine that she turned down Halle's role in *Monster's Ball*. "I wasn't going to be a prostitute on film," Bassett was quoted as saying. "I couldn't do that because it's such a stereotype about black women and sexuality." She went on to say: "Film is forever. It's about putting something out there you can be proud of ten years later. I mean, Meryl Streep won Oscars without that."

I talked to Daniels about Bassett's comment after the story broke. He denied that Bassett was ever offered the lead role in *Monster's Ball*. He said the filmmakers expressed an interest in meeting with her and that was all (the meeting never happened, he said). Said Daniels: "To me, it sounds like Angela Bassett's got sour grapes or something, you know what I mean? Get your own Oscar, baby."

The night of her win, Halle and her husband were seen closing down the Elton John/*InStyle* party. It was 2:30 A.M. She was holding the Oscar in one hand and gripping Benet's hand with the other (she would later take both Benet and the Oscar to bed that night, for what she described as her one and only "three-way").

Around 4:00 A.M. she called Daniels in his room at the Chateau Marmont.

Halle told him Nelson Mandela had talked to her.

Daniels said he couldn't believe this was all happening.

They both cried into the telephone.

Halle had conquered Hollywood.

The world was next.

"I'm stronger than I ever thought I could be. I am capable of weathering the worst of storms."

—HALLE BERRY

Afterword,
or Live Another Day

THREE DAYS AFTER BECOMING THE FIRST AFRICAN-American woman to win a best actress Oscar, Halle Berry was still on the rise.

On a sun-drenched beach in Cardiz, a town in southern Spain, Berry was rising out of the water. She was dressed in a skin tight, Day-Glo orange bikini, and she had a large knife sheathed on her side. Cameras flashed. The whole tableau was a media opportunity, a staged flashback set to resemble a famous scene from *Dr. No* (1962), the Bond film that gave birth to the whole series (and also the first Bond film Halle ever saw). Halle was a Bond girl now, set to play Jinx, a villain, opposite Pierce Brosnan, who was back for his fourth time as James Bond in the upcoming 007 film *Die Another Day*.

In that first Bond flick, Ursula Andress, playing the suggestively named Honeychile Ryder, famously rose from the waters of the Caribbean in a similar suit, with a similar knife, seducing the first James Bond, Sean Connery. Now, forty years later, in the twentieth Bond film, Halle was recapturing the same seductive magic.

Unfortunately, the Atlantic in April is not as warm as the Caribbean at any time of the year, and soon Halle was away from the cameras and hugging a hot water bottle for warmth. Despite the chill, the assembled press had gotten the message: Bond was back, and the new movie promised to be hotter than ever.

Going from Oscar-winning leading lady to knife-wielding Bond girl, on the surface, seemed an odd choice for Halle. That first step after Oscar gold is always the toughest one, especially for young actresses. Life after the Academy Award is often as empty as the envelope the Oscar announcement was delivered in. After Mira Sorvino won the Oscar for best supporting actress in 1996 for her role in Woody Allen's *Mighty Aphrodite,* her very next film was the drug drama flop *Sweet Nothing* (Total box-office gross: $79,249—that's right, it didn't even make six figures). After Angelina Jolie won best actress in 2000 for *Girl, Interrupted* she released the flop *Gone in 60 Seconds,* the disappointing *Tomb Raider,* the critically panned *Original Sin,* and the shamefully unfunny purported comedy *Life or Something Like It.* You could use any one of those three movie titles to craft a mean joke about how Jolie's career looked post-Oscar.

In 1991, the first time I interviewed Halle, she told me she wanted to write her own scripts and create her own vehicles. Back then she was even writing her own thriller: a screenplay titled "Inside Out." Halle told me then: "Someone has got to be a pioneer and get it done, keep trying when doors are slammed in your face." Now that Halle had opened doors for herself with an Oscar, she was going on through. Halle, with Bond, had a safe bet—the Bond franchise is one of the most popular film series in the world. Each of the last three Bond films (all made since Brosnan signed on), had grossed more than $100 million in the United States, and millions more abroad. It wasn't a question if the film would be a hit, it was merely a question how big a hit it was going to be. Halle and her manager wanted to ride some of that success. After all, she had something to prove. Not to critics—her *Monster's Ball* win had answered them. And not to herself—ever since she convinced Spike Lee to let her play a crackhead in *Jungle Fever* she had had faith in her own acting abilities.

No, Halle wanted to prove something to Hollywood moneymen, the producers with the power to green-light projects, all those studio executives who were constantly fretting over her box-office potential and saying things like "black doesn't travel." Hollywood, more than ever, was a global business. According to the weekly publication *Screen International,* in 2000, nearly 46 percent of the studios' total profits came from sales abroad. Harrison Ford, Arnold Schwarzenegger, Bruce Willis—sure, they were old guys now. And, of course, they were white guys. But they sold pictures overseas to people who were not old and not white—people knew their work, people knew their faces, even if they didn't speak their language. Who the heck was Halle Berry? The studio execs would say it to her manager's face: Black didn't travel.

So for *Die Another Day,* Halle traveled. The production shot in Hong Kong, in Cuba, in Hawaii, in Iceland, in England. She especially relished her time in London, enjoying the traditional treat of scones and clotted cream during afternoon tea (though she avoided sugar and chocolate because of her diabetes). While abroad, she made sure to bring the pleasures of home with her: She had Kraft Zesty Italian salad dressing shipped to her—it's her favorite, and she couldn't find it in London. She also kept her trailer decorated with pictures of her stepdaughter, India, her husband, and her beloved Maltese dogs Polly and Willy.

Even before the film wrapped, Halle was courting the international press: talking about how eager she was to let go of herself and play a villain, joking about how she wished her character could be named something sexier and Bond-like, such as "Cinnamon Buns" (as a joke, she was affectionately called the nickname on the set). Halle even endured a tough shoot for Bond: Pierce Brosnan injured his knee during filming and at one point Halle suffered an inflamed eye thanks to wind-blown dust (there were rumors that a stunt grenade had injured her eye with shrapnel, but producers denied it).

The Bond franchise is nothing if not worldly: Ian Fleming, who wrote the novels on which the movies are based, was a former intelligence officer with Britain's Royal Navy. His first Bond book, *Casino Royale* (1953), initially had a printing of just 4,750 copies; however, the series soon became an international sensation—in 1961, John F. Kennedy cited *From Russia With Love* as one of his ten favorite books. The series was born of the Cold

War; as the British empire faded, 007 gave Anglophiles everywhere someone and something to believe in. *Dr. No* (1962), the first Bond movie, was filmed in Jamaica while the island was still under British control; by the time the film was released, Jamaica was independent. The British had lost their holdings, but they still had their fantasies.

And what a fantasy figure Bond was. He had style: martinis shaken, not stirred. He had a memorable way of introducing himself: "Bond. James Bond." He had gadgets: a cigarlike device that provides oxygen in *Thunderball* (1965), a BMW with machine guns and rockets in *Tomorrow Never Dies* (1997). He had a way with words: In *Goldfinger* (1964), after a character is electrocuted, Bond says "Shocking! Positively shocking!" In *Diamonds Are Forever* (1971), when a woman introduces herself as "Plenty O'Toole," Bond answers smoothly: "But of course you are." And, naturally, rightfully, inevitably, Bond has women, lots of them, all colorfully and usually suggestively named. Tiffany Case (played by Jill St. John) in *Diamonds Are Forever,* Xenia Onatopp (Famke Janssen) in *GoldenEye* (1995), and of course, Pussy Galore (Honor Blackman) in *Goldfinger.* When she introduces herself, Bond says, "I must be dreaming."

Before *Maxim* magazine, before the Victoria's Secret catalog, before Beyonce Knowles in the Austin Powers sequel, there was the Bond girl. Spun out of cigar smoke, lingerie, and Teflon, Bond girls are the ultimate male fantasy: beautiful, dangerous, sophisticated, and, most important, usually available. Their name is a kind of misnomer—they are never girls, they are always women; and although the actresses who play them are called "Bond girls," their connections to him never last more than one movie. Kim Basinger was a Bond girl *(Never Say Never Again)*. Michelle Yeoh was a Bond girl *(Tomorrow Never Dies)*. Jane Seymour was a Bond girl *(Live and Let Die)*. Talented actress after talented actress—and some not so talented—over the years have decided that there's merit in immersing oneself in the patriarchal celluloid dream that is 007. Even the filmmakers behind Bond understood they were selling retrograde illusion. In *GoldenEye,* Dame Judi Dench, who plays Bond's supervisor "M," tells Brosnan's 007 that she considers him a "sexist, misogynist, dinosaur." And of course she's right.

Bond survives because he fills a particular cinematic and psychic need. The Cold War was a good war for the movies because it was all talk no action. And so the movies provided the action: the firing, the explosions, the body count—*Dr. Strangelove, The Manchurian Candidate, The Hunt for Red October, The Sum of All Fears.* Russian and American troops never fought a single direct battle in real life; in the movies, however, a thousand battles were won and lost. In the nineties and 2000 and beyond, even though the Cold War is over, Bond continues to fight. In *Live and Let Die* he took on a Harlem crime boss (sparking some protest from African-American groups). In *Tomorrow Never Dies,* Bond clashed with an evil media baron. And the latest Bond adventure, *Die Another Day,* evokes the conflict between North and South Korea. Sometimes Bond's battles are based on front-page news, sometimes they are last week's news; it doesn't matter who he is fighting these days, only that he is still in the fray, that there is still some spirit left in the old dreams of hegemony. Bond isn't really a Cold Warrior. Bond is about Male Bonding. And that's forever.

So now Bond's war is Halle's War. If he conquers the world, so will she. First she wants America. The U.S. movie-going audience is becoming more diverse: According to the Motion Picture Association of America, in 2001 more than 39 percent of the American moviegoing audience was Latino, African American, or Asian. Unfortunately, for filmmakers of color, all those folks aren't typically going to see films with Latinos, African Americans, and Asians in them. *Monster's Ball* made about as much over its entire run as the last Bond picture made in its first weekend. Many more moviegoers, with *Die Another Day*, will be introduced to Halle Berry for the first time. And many of the moviegoers who see the film in Iceland and Spain and Britain and Hong Kong and everywhere else it plays will be introduced to Halle, most for the first time. For Bond, Halle will travel. And after Bond, she may be able to keep traveling even more.

Perhaps it's fitting that a guy like Bond should take Halle on a trip around the world. Halle's troubles with men have been well documented: at least one boyfriend abused her, and she was famously divorced from David Justice. Halle's problems with her father are well known:

He was, by her account, cruel to her and her mother, he abandoned her as a child, and he was a heavy drinker. Bond, in some ways, is like some of those men in Halle's past: He's a drinker, a rogue, a man with a secret life, a man who usually hurts those he loves. By one estimate, of Bond's sixty on-screen paramours, twenty-one of them die. The main difference between Bond and most of the men who have populated Halle's life is that Bond usually ends up saving the planet, while the men in her life usually end up just wrecking her world.

In the summer of 2002, newspapers around the United States carried the story that Halle's husband, Eric Benet, had cheated on her and that he had checked into The Meadows, a rehabilitation clinic in Wickenburg, Arizona, that has programs that deal with sexual addiction. Wickenburg is a small community (population: 4,500) where gossip spreads fast, and Halle, Benet, and the couple's daughter, India, were spotted around the town, dining at local restaurants such as Anita's Cocina. ("Her bill was forty dollars, and she left a tip of ten bucks," said Jessie Solper, a waitress who served Halle at that restaurant.) Wickenburg residents who ran into Halle and Benet say the couple appeared composed, and were unfailingly polite to people they met. Will Halle's latest marriage last? Her union with Justice withered on the vine. With Benet, she seems to be taking a more proactive stance. Reportedly, Benet checked into The Meadows at her urging.

Halle may play a Bond girl in the movies, but she's far from one in real life. Halle, in a way, has functioned as her *own* James Bond, saving herself and her *own* life, repeatedly. Bond girls have sometimes waited for their secret agent man to rescue them or to ravish them. Not Halle. She has made her own opportunities: badgering Spike Lee for a juicy role in *Jungle Fever,* convincing Steven Spielberg to cast her in *The Flintstones* and thus integrate Bedrock, convincing the filmmakers behind *Monster's Ball* that she wasn't "too pretty" for the part and going on to win a groundbreaking, historic Oscar.

Halle has had plenty of rough moments in her career and plenty of reasons to give up, but she's established a theme in her life and she's stuck to it:

You can't change your past. But you can always make history.